WITTGENSTEIN

Also by A. J. Ayer

WITTGENSTEIN

A. J. AYER

THE UNIVERSITY OF CHICAGO PRESS

Published by arrangement with Random House, Inc.

The University of Chicago Press, Chicago 60637

95 94 93 92 91 90 89 88 87 86   5 4 3 2 1

Library of Congress Cataloging in Publication Data

Ayer, A. J. (Alfred Jules), 1910–
  Wittgenstein.

  Bibliography: p.
  Includes index.
  1. Wittgenstein, Ludwig, 1889–1951.   I. Title.
B3376.W564A94   1986   192   86-11278
ISBN 0-226-03337-6 (pbk.)

TO
PETER STRAWSON

CONTENTS

PREFACE

The purpose of this book is set out at the beginning of its first chapter. It explains among other things why I have for the most part chosen to approach Wittgenstein's writings directly, avoiding confrontation with the numerous and often talented expositors who have preceded me. In my rejection of Wittgenstein's so-called private-language argument, and in the chapter devoted to his book *On Certainty*, I have borrowed freely from previously published work of my own. I apologize for this to those of my readers who detect the repetitions.

It remains only for me to thank Mrs Guida Crowley, once again, for typing the manuscript and helping me to correct the proofs, and my wife for her assistance in compiling the index.

A.J. Ayer
51 York Street
London W1

August 1984

INTRODUCTION: BIOGRAPHICAL SKETCH

So many books have been written about the philosophy of Ludwig Wittgenstein that an excuse is needed for adding to their number. My defence is that, while his name has become quite widely known, especially in recent years, there appears to be very little understanding of his work, outside the circle of professional philosophers. Within this circle itself, there is no very general agreement as to the importance of his views or even their correct interpretation. Some painstaking commentaries have been written, but besides their mutual disagreement on points of central interest they deal only with special phases of his work. There are at least two very good attempts to provide a general survey of his philosophy, one by David Pears, contributed to the Fontana Modern Masters series in 1971, the other by Anthony Kenny, in a Pelican book appearing in 1973, and I am indebted to them both. I judge, however, that neither of them would convey very much to a reader who did not already have considerable training in philosophy. My object is to give an account of the successive phases of Wittgenstein's thought which will be accessible to such a reader, and still be of some interest to my professional colleagues. I claim no special qualification for this difficult undertaking. I had a slight personal acquaintance with Wittgenstein, which was predominantly friendly. Though I was never a pupil of his, I was very strongly influenced by his early work. I have not, however, adhered to the Wittgensteinian cult which has grown up since his death. If I did not think him an important philosopher, I should not be writing this book. All the same, my admiration for him falls short of idolatry.

Ludwig Wittgenstein was born in Vienna on 26 April, 1889. The Wittgensteins were of Jewish descent but Ludwig's grandfather had been converted to Protestantism. His mother was a Roman Catholic and Ludwig himself was baptized into the Catholic Church. He retained a respect for religion, at least in some form, though he was not a churchgoer in adult life. His father held a prominent position in the Austrian iron and steel industries and the family was rich. There were nine children of whom Ludwig was the youngest. Of his four brothers three committed suicide. The other, Paul Wittgenstein, having lost an arm in the First World War, achieved fame as a one-armed concert pianist.

After being educated at home until he was fourteen, Ludwig Wittgenstein went to school at Linz for three years and then studied engineering in Berlin. In 1908 he came to England and enrolled as a research student at Manchester University. He became interested in aeronautics and is rumoured to have designed the prototype of a jet engine and a propeller for aeroplanes. His interest extended to mathematics and then to its foundations. As a result he read Bertrand Russell's *Principles of Mathematics*. Through Russell's book, Wittgenstein learned of the existence of Gottlob Frege, then a little-known professor at the University of Jena, but now widely esteemed as the greatest logician since Aristotle. Wittgenstein was enthralled by Frege's writings and visited him at Jena in 1911. He then took Frege's advice to study logic under Bertrand Russell at Cambridge. Russell was then a lecturer at Trinity College and Wittgenstein spent five terms there in the years 1912-13, first as an undergraduate and then as an advanced student. From the outset he made a strong impression both on Russell and on the other outstanding Cambridge philosopher, G.E. Moore. They procured his election to the secret society of the Apostles, a favour for which Wittgenstein was not at all grateful, and in a letter to Lowes Dickinson, reprinted in the first volume of Russell's *Autobiography*, Russell described Wittgenstein as 'much the most apostolic and the ablest person I have come across since Moore'. Russell was nearly seventeen years older than Wittgenstein and Moore sixteen, but they both treated him as at least their equal. In fact, when Wittgenstein left Cambridge and went to live in Norway in an isolated hut which he had built for himself, Moore visited him there in the spring of 1914 and took notes at his dictation. It was also the severity of Wittgenstein's criticism that caused Russell in 1913 to abandon a book that he was writing on the theory of knowledge. In a letter written to Lady

Ottoline Morrell in 1916 Russell confessed that Wittgenstein's on-slaught had driven him to despair and made him think that he could not hope ever again to do fundamental work in philosophy.[1] Fortunately, Russell recovered quickly enough to deliver the Lowell lectures in Boston early in 1914, which were published under the title of *Our Knowledge of the External World*.

When war broke out later in the year, Wittgenstein at once enlisted as a machine-gunner in the Austrian army, becoming an officer in 1915. He fought mostly on the Eastern front but was transferred to the Southern front in 1918 and captured by the Italians in November 1918. They kept him a prisoner for several months after the Armistice and it was not until August 1919 that he was able to return to Austria.

His father's death in 1912 had made Wittgenstein a very rich man. Before the war he had been very generous with his money, making an anonymous grant to the Cambridge logician W.E. Johnson and also donating a large sum anonymously, from which the poet Rilke profited among others, for the promotion of literature. His own tastes were frugal and at some point during the war, possibly as the result of reading Tolstoy on the Gospels, he decided to divest himself of all his money. He gave it not to the poor, whom it might corrupt, but to the members of his family who were already so rich that it would not harm them.

Throughout the war Wittgenstein had carried notebooks with him which he filled with his philosophical reflections and when he was on leave in Vienna in August 1918 he assembled a selection of these notes into a short treatise. He took this treatise with him into captivity and sent copies of it to Frege and to Bertrand Russell. Frege could make nothing of the work but Russell thought well of it. Its appeal to him may have been greater because it embroidered themes which he had discussed with Wittgenstein before the war. They had completely lost touch with one another during the interval, as is shown by a footnote in Russell's *Introduction to Mathematical Philosophy*, written in 1918, while Russell himself was serving a prison sentence for libelling the American army. The footnote, which was strangely not excised from later editions of the book, runs: 'The importance of "tautology" for a definition of mathematics was pointed out to me by my former pupil

---

[1] Autobiography, vol. II, p. 57.

Ludwig Wittgenstein, who was working on the problem. I do not know whether he has solved it, or even whether he is alive or dead.'[1]

Russell discovered that Wittgenstein was not dead from a postcard which Wittgenstein sent him in February 1919. They started a correspondence and agreed, after Wittgenstein's release, to meet in Holland as soon as possible to discuss Wittgenstein's manuscript and arrange for its publication, with an introduction by Russell. The difficulty then arose that Wittgenstein, having given all his money away, could not afford the fare from Vienna to The Hague and was too proud to let Russell pay it for him. The problem was solved by Russell's buying some furniture which Wittgenstein had left in store at Cambridge and sending Wittgenstein the proceeds.

Wittgenstein had entitled his treatise *Logisch-philosophische Abhandlung*. The book was short, amounting in all to some 20,000 words. It was written in numbered paragraphs, according to a decimal system in which, for example, the proposition numbered 3.001 is a comment on proposition number 3, the propositions numbered 3.01, 3.02, 3.03 take the argument three small steps forward, 3.031 is a comment on 3.03, 3.1 makes a further advance and so on. The main headings run from 1 to 7. The German style is elegant but the plan of the book makes it very elliptical, justifying C.D. Broad's reference to 'the highly syncopated pipings of Herr Wittgenstein's flute'.

Russell relates in the second volume of his *Autobiography* that he and Wittgenstein spent a week at The Hague 'arguing his book line by line'.[2] Nevertheless when Wittgenstein read Russell's introduction he complained that Russell had not understood him. In a biographical sketch, which G.H. von Wright, to whom I am much indebted, published in conjunction with a revealing memoir by Norman Malcolm, one of Wittgenstein's most devoted pupils, it is asserted that at this point 'Wittgenstein turned his back on the whole undertaking',[3] but this must be taken to mean no more than that he did not exert himself to find a publisher. When Russell informed him in 1921 that he had arranged for the work to appear in the final number of Ostwald's *Annalen der Naturphilosophie*, he expressed pleasure at the news,

---

[1] p. 205 fn.
[2] Autobiography, vol. II, p. 130.
[3] *Ludwig Wittgenstein: A Memoir by Norman Malcolm, with a Biographical Sketch by G.H. von Wright*, p. 11.

while speaking of Ostwald as a charlatan, who needed to be watched in case he made even the slightest alteration to the text.

In the following year the book was accepted by Kegan Paul for their International Library of Psychology, Philosophy, and Scientific Method, which C.K. Ogden edited. Russell's English introduction was preserved and the device was adopted of printing Wittgenstein's German text and an English translation, made by Ogden with some help from F.P. Ramsey, on facing pages. The book was called *Tractatus Logico-Philosophicus*, a title said to have been suggested by G.E. Moore. It has most commonly been referred to simply as the *Tractatus*. It contained a note by Ogden, saying that the proofs of the translation and the version of the original which Ostwald had published had been very carefully revised by the author himself. Nevertheless the translation was later found to be defective in some respects, and when the International Library was revived under my editorship by what had become the firm of Routledge and Kegan Paul, I commissioned a new translation by David Pears and Brian McGuinness. Russell allowed his original introduction to be reprinted, a few minor alterations, mainly of punctuation, were made in the German text and the *Tractatus* appeared in its new guise in 1961. An enthusiastic but not uncritical notice of the original version had been contributed to *Mind* in 1923 by F.P. Ramsey, who was still only twenty years old. Ramsey was one of the few philosophers with whom Wittgenstein was willing to argue on equal terms, and his death in 1930 was a very great loss to Cambridge philosophy. I shall try to elicit the message and estimate the value of the *Tractatus* later on.

Wittgenstein in 1919 believed that the *Tractatus* supplied the definitive solution to all the problems of philosophy, so far as they were soluble, and therefore turned his attention to other pursuits. He attended a teachers' training college, and from 1920 till 1926 taught in elementary schools in the districts of Schneeberg and Semmering in Lower Austria. He took his duties seriously and seems on the whole to have been liked by his pupils but did not get on well with their parents, mostly local farmers, or with his fellow teachers. A priest in the neighbourhood was his only friend. One of the villages at which he taught was Trattenbach and Wittgenstein wrote to Russell in October 1921 that he was surrounded, as ever, by odiousness and baseness, adding that while he knew that human beings were not worth much anywhere the people at Trattenbach were much less good for anything and more irresponsible than anywhere else. Russell, who was then a visiting professor at Peking, and as captivated by the Chinese as he had been disillusioned by the Russian communist leaders whom he had met in Moscow, replied that he found this proposition improbable. Wittgenstein agreed that the people of Trattenbach were not worse than all the rest of mankind but explained that Trattenbach was a particularly insignificant place in Austria and that the Austrians had sunk so wretchedly low since the war that it was too sad to talk about. Nevertheless he continued to teach in the area until a group of parents brought a legal action against him for treating their children with undue physical severity. Wittgenstein won the action but relinquished his post. He had in the meantime compiled a German glossary for use in elementary schools. This came out in 1926 and was the only book apart from the *Tractatus* that Wittgenstein published in his lifetime.

After ceasing to be a schoolteacher Wittgenstein worked for a short time as a gardener's assistant at the monastery of Hütteldorf near Vienna. Von Wright reports that Wittgenstein thought seriously on several occasions of becoming a monk but could not muster enough religious faith. Instead he spent the next two years designing and supervising the construction of a house in Vienna for his sister Mrs Stonborough. The house which was built of concrete, glass and steel was severely functional, somewhat in the Bauhaus style. It has now been adapted to serve as the Bulgarian Embassy. So far as I know this was the only building that Wittgenstein constructed, though from 1933 to 1938 he was listed in the Vienna city directory as an architect. According to von Wright, he also executed a piece of sculpture, 'the head of a girl or an elf',[1] in what von Wright describes as a Classical Greek style.

In 1923, while he was teaching at the village of Puchberg, and again in 1924, Wittgenstein was visited by Ramsey and, in 1925, Maynard Keynes made it financially possible for him to visit Cambridge, but his interest in philosophy did not fully revive until he met and made friends with Moritz Schlick, a German who had come from Kiel to Vienna in 1922 to occupy Ernst Mach's old University Chair of the

[1] *Ludwig Wittgenstein: A Memoir by Norman Malcolm, with a Biographical Sketch by G. H. von Wright*, p. 11.

History and Philosophy of the Inductive Sciences. Schlick was the organizer and chairman of a group of philosophers, mathematicians and scientists which became known as the Vienna Circle. It held regular weekly meetings from 1925 until 1936 when Schlick's murder by one of his former pupils and the Nazi threat to Austria led to its dissolution. Schlick was an early admirer of the *Tractatus*, which he introduced to the Circle, and would have liked also to enlist its author. But Wittgenstein refused. He did however consent to discuss philosophy with Schlick, Rudolf Carnap and Friedrich Waismann. According to Carnap, these meetings started in 1927 and continued, so far as Carnap was concerned, until 1929, when Wittgenstein broke off relations with him. One reason for this may have been that he suspected Carnap of plagiarism. He always had an almost morbid fear of anyone's purloining or misrepresenting his ideas. He remained on good terms with Schlick and also with Waismann, whom he saw regularly on his visits to Vienna in the early 1930s and used as a touchstone for his new theories.

In 1929 Wittgenstein was persuaded, mainly by Ramsey, to return to Cambridge. He submitted the *Tractatus* as his thesis for a Ph.D. and was examined by Moore and Russell. Moore's report is said to have been: 'It is my personal opinion that Mr Wittgenstein's thesis is a work of genius; but, be that as it may, it is certainly well up to the standard required for the Cambridge degree of Doctor of Philosophy.'

Wittgenstein duly received his doctorate and at the end of the following year was elected to a Research Fellowship at Trinity, tenable for five years and in fact extended to a sixth. He had by then started to compose a dissertation of about eight hundred pages entitled *Philosophische Grammatik*. Another manuscript which he submitted for a grant was entitled *Philosophische Bemerkungen (Philosophical Remarks)*. Russell is quoted by von Wright as saying of part of it: 'The theories contained in this new work of Wittgenstein's are novel, very original and indubitably important. Whether they are true, I do not know. As a logician, who likes simplicity, I should wish to think that they are not, but from what I have read of them I am quite sure that he ought to have an opportunity to work them out, since when completed they may easily prove to constitute a whole new philosophy.'[1]

[1] ibid., p. 13 fn.

Like the bulk of Wittgenstein's work, the *Philosophische Grammatik* and the *Philosophical Remarks* were published posthumously. The only article of Wittgenstein's to appear in his lifetime was a piece entitled 'Some Remarks on Logical Form', which was included in the *Supplementary Proceedings of the Aristotelian Society* for 1929 as having been delivered at the Joint Session of the Aristotelian Society and the Mind Association for that year. Normally such pieces are contributions to symposia, but in this case there was no other symposiast, and Wittgenstein neither read nor commented on his paper but talked about mathematical infinity instead.

We have it on the authority of Moore that Wittgenstein started lecturing at Cambridge in January 1930. He gave one lecture and one discussion class every week in each of the three terms that make up the academic year. There was an audience of about twenty persons. Wittgenstein did not admit those whom he called 'tourists' to his lectures or classes. One was expected to attend regularly if one came at all. Though he was already a professor, Moore himself attended all the discussion classes and with the exception of two terms all the lectures that Wittgenstein gave in the period 1930 to 1933, and took very full notes. They occupy over seventy pages of Moore's *Philosophical Papers*, for the rest a collection of Moore's own essays, most of them previously published, which appeared posthumously in 1959, a year after Moore's death. These notes, which ranged over the philosophy of logic, the philosophy of language, the theory of knowledge and even so far as ethics and aesthetics, were critical of positions that Wittgenstein had adopted in the *Tractatus*. The same is true of the notes which Waismann made of the conversations which he had with Wittgenstein a year or two earlier in Vienna. These were edited by Brian McGuinness and published as late as 1979.

The best indication of the ways in which Wittgenstein's thought was developing in the 1930s is to be found in two sets of notes, one of which Wittgenstein dictated to his class in the academic year 1933-4, and the other which he dictated to two of his pupils in 1934-5. They were known respectively as *The Blue Book* and *The Brown Book* because of the colours of the wrappers in which they were bound, and they were published under the title of *The Blue and Brown Books* in 1958, seven years after Wittgenstein's death. Owing to their provenance, these notes appear only in English, whereas Wittgenstein's other posthumously published texts nearly all follow the model of the *Tractatus*, with Wittgenstein's own German musings confronting an English translation carried out or commissioned by his literary executors.

Both the *Blue* and the *Brown* books were designed primarily for Wittgenstein's own use. They were not intended to make his current ideas more generally known. This was particularly true of *The Brown Book*, of which, according to its editor Rush Rhees, only three typed copies were made, and shown by Wittgenstein 'only to very close friends and pupils'. But some of these failed to keep the secret. Further copies were made and some of them even found their way to Oxford, following the *Blue Book* which had never been quite so closely guarded. Wittgenstein even sent a copy of it to Russell about two years after it was first produced. It is not known how Russell reacted to it. He never entirely lost his respect for Wittgenstein, though he was increasingly opposed to the tenor of Wittgenstein's later works.

In 1935 Wittgenstein ceased to treat Waismann as a collaborator. This was all the more of a disappointment to Waismann as for the past five years he had been working on a book which was intended to be a vehicle for the expression of Wittgenstein's discoveries. Under the title *Logik, Sprache, Philosophie*, to which I have to confess that I was indebted for my own *Language, Truth and Logic*, it was advertised as early as 1930, as the first in a series of volumes sponsored by the Vienna Circle. It may even have been completed in 1931, but it never appeared and the series, which contained important works by Schlick, Philipp Frank, Karl Popper and Otto Neurath, began with the number two. Waismann never succeeded in reshaping his book into a form which satisfied Wittgenstein and never published it in his lifetime, though a version of it, edited by Brian McGuinness and others, appeared with Schlick's original preface in 1976, seventeen years after Waismann's death. It can be seen as the forerunner of a book of his published in an English translation in 1965 under the title *Principles of Linguistic Philosophy*, but by then enough of Wittgenstein's own later work had been published to rob Waismann's book of most of the interest that it might otherwise have had.

For a few years at least Waismann remained loyal to Wittgenstein.

As late as 1938, in a paper entitled 'The Relevance of Psychology to Logic', he added the footnote: 'I wish to emphasize my indebtedness to Dr Wittgenstein to whom I owe not only a great part of the views expressed in this paper but also my whole method of dealing with philosophical questions. Although I hope that the views expressed here are in agreement with those of Dr Wittgenstein, I do not wish to ascribe to him any responsibility for them.'[1] Such acknowledgements and disclaimers were common form among Wittgenstein's disciples. This particular paper of Waismann's was a contribution to a symposium, in which Bertrand Russell and R.B. Braithwaite were the other participants, and appeared in the *Supplementary Proceedings of the Aristotelian Society* for 1938. By that time Waismann, who was Jewish, had been forced to flee with his family from Vienna by the advent of the Nazis and had made his way to Cambridge. His presence there, however, was an annoyance to Wittgenstein and Waismann found refuge in Oxford which elected him to readerships first in the philosophy of mathematics and then in the philosophy of science. His later papers, which were written in English, are, at least in one case, even critical of Wittgenstein, to whom they pay no further tribute, though they are seldom wholly free of Wittgenstein's influence.

Wittgenstein himself had visited Russia in 1935 and had seriously thought of settling there, attracted perhaps by the austerity of its form of life. No doubt there was already enough evidence of Stalin's tyranny to deter him. After his Trinity fellowship had expired he retreated to his hut in Norway and worked on a book which he intended to publish, the celebrated *Philosophische Untersuchungen*, better known under the title of its English translation as *Philosophical Investigations*, or more simply as *The Investigations*. The first part, which was completed by 1945, consists of 693 numbered paragraphs and is furnished with a preface, describing it as the precipitate of investigations which had occupied the author for the past sixteen years. It is not clear why he did not then arrange for the publication of the book, but a reason suggested by its eventual editors, Elizabeth Anscombe and Rush Rhees, is that he was dissatisfied with the formulation of many of the later paragraphs and would have replaced them with material taken from

---

[1] Friedrich Waismann, *Philosophical Papers*, p. 80.

the second and much shorter part of the total work as we now have it. This second part consists of unnumbered paragraphs, arranged in order by the editors, and appended to the original *Investigations*. The notes of which it consists were compiled by Wittgenstein in the years 1947-9. The whole assemblage was translated by Elizabeth Anscombe and published in 1953, two years after Wittgenstein's death, in the same format as the *Tractatus*, with the German text and its English translation on facing pages.

Wittgenstein resumed lecturing at Cambridge in 1937, though his Fellowship at Trinity was not renewed until 1939 when Moore retired from his Professorship and Wittgenstein was elected to succeed him. Norman Malcolm, who first came to Cambridge from America in 1938, gives a very good account in his Memoir of Wittgenstein's appearance, manner and lecturing technique. It tallies with my own recollection of him as short, slender and tense, with penetrating blue eyes, speaking English fluently with very little accent but occasional lapses of idiom. His rooms were possibly the same as those that he occupied when Gilbert Ryle first took me to see him in 1932, situated at the very top of a high staircase, the sitting-room like a monk's cell, with no ornament, a table and chair for Wittgenstein's own use, no armchairs but two deckchairs brought out for visitors. Malcolm reports that a supply of chairs was kept in the passage outside for the use of Wittgenstein's audience. By 1939, when Malcolm first attended them, his lectures had all turned into classes. The classes took place twice a week from five to seven in the evening. Wittgenstein is described by Malcolm as sitting in a plain wooden chair in the middle of the room. He spoke without notes and gave the impression of wrestling with his thoughts, often falling into silences which no one dared to interrupt. Sometimes he put questions to members of his audience and drew them into a discussion, with the object of developing some point of his own. I do not think that he encouraged them to take the lead, or that he cared to have his assertions contradicted. He could be impatient with any show of misunderstanding and brutal to anyone who made a remark that he considered stupid. He had favourites, of whom Malcolm was one, but did not spare them. Malcolm writes of an occasion at the Moral Science Club when Moore read a paper which Wittgenstein criticized in the ensuing discussion. Malcolm thought that Wittgenstein's criticism had been unfair to Moore and said so. I continue the story in Malcolm's own words: 'Directly after the meeting ended, and while people were still standing about, Wittgenstein walked up to me and said, eyes blazing with anger, "If you knew anything at all you would know that I am never unfair to anyone. This proves that you have understood absolutely nothing of my lectures." He turned and walked away; I was thunderstruck.'[1] It should be added that when Wittgenstein learned a few days later that Malcolm had succumbed to influenza, he at once went round to his lodgings and helped to take care of him.

His classes always left Wittgenstein in a state of nervous exhaustion. According to Malcolm, he used to rush off to the cinema, if possible getting a member of the class to accompany him. He chose to sit in the front row so as to be more thoroughly immersed in the film. He had a strong preference for American films, especially the brassier sort of musical comedy, with such leading ladies as Carmen Miranda and Betty Hutton. Although he took British citizenship after the Germans annexed Austria, he was predominantly hostile to what he conceived to be the British way of life and this was expressed, among other ways, in his antipathy to British films. He went so far as to quarrel with Gilbert Ryle because Ryle refused to agree that a good British film was not even a possibility.

Ryle was one of the few people who both liked Wittgenstein and did not fear him. The Cambridge economist Piero Sraffa, who convinced Wittgenstein that there were faults in the *Tractatus*, was another. C.D. Broad did not fear him but disliked him. He believed, what von Wright reports that Wittgenstein himself suspected, that 'his influence as a teacher was, on the whole, harmful to the development of independent minds in his disciples'.[2] I was myself sufficiently detached to be both annoyed and amused by their imitation of his mannerisms. In the autobiography which he supplied for *The Philosophy of G.E. Moore*, Moore wrote of Wittgenstein that: 'When I did get to know him, I soon came to feel that he was much cleverer at philosophy than I was and not only cleverer, but also more profound, and with a much better insight into the sort of inquiry which was really important

---

[1] *Ludwig Wittgenstein: A Memoir by Norman Malcolm, with a Biographical Sketch by G.H. von Wright*, p. 34.
[2] ibid., p. 19.

and best worth pursuing, and into the best method of pursuing such inquiries.'[1] I think that this was a view that Wittgenstein shared, though he admired Moore's character. In the case of anyone less noble than Moore it might have aroused resentment, but in fact I have no reason to suppose that it did. Nor do I know how far von Wright was speaking for himself when he wrote in his sketch of Wittgenstein: 'I believe that most of those who loved him and had his friendship also feared him.'[2]

With one or two exceptions, such as the mathematician G.H. Hardy, Wittgenstein avoided the other Fellows of Trinity and took as small a part as possible in Cambridge academic life. He confessed to a need for affection and sought it from his younger disciples, whom he sometimes succeeded in discouraging from becoming philosophers. He was interested at least in some aspects of the works of Russell and Moore, but in general he held a low opinion of contemporary philosophy. He had a particular fondness for the stories in the American detective magazines published by Street and Smith, and I do not think that he was joking when he compared them favourably to the articles in *Mind*, writing to Malcolm who had sent him a batch from America: 'Your mags are wonderful. How people can read *Mind* if they could read Street & Smith beats me. If philosophy has anything to do with wisdom there's certainly not a grain of that in *Mind*, & quite often a grain in the detective stories.'[3]

Wittgenstein was not entirely dismissive of the philosophers of the past, but his reading of them was markedly eclectic. As a boy he was strongly influenced by Schopenhauer's principal work *The World as Will and Representation*, and we shall see that this influence persists in the *Tractatus*, though the only philosophers to whom he acknowledges a debt in the *Tractatus* are Frege and Russell. The book contains a passing reference to Kant and has been thought by some critics to display a Kantian approach, but there is no evidence that Wittgenstein made any serious study of Kant's writings and his knowledge of Kant was most probably filtered through Schopenhauer. He told von Wright that he could make little of either Spinoza or Hume, though the interpretation which the Vienna Circle put upon the *Tractatus* allied him

[1] p. 33.
[2] op. cit., pp. 18-19.
[3] *Ludwig Wittgenstein: A Memoir by Norman Malcolm, with a Biographical Sketch by G.H. von Wright*, p. 36.

very closely to Hume. We shall see, however, that there is good reason to doubt whether this interpretation was correct. He credited Berkeley with being deep, which was one of his highest terms of praise, but I do not think that this verdict, though just, was based on a thorough study of Berkeley's writings. A philosopher whom he is known to have read and enjoyed is Plato, though there are no signs in his own work of Platonic ideas. Von Wright suggests that he may have found Plato's temperament congenial.

Von Wright's conclusion, which there is no reason to doubt, is that 'Wittgenstein received deeper impressions from some writers in the borderland between philosophy, religion and poetry than from the philosophers, in the restricted sense of the word. Among the former are St Augustine, Kierkegaard, Dostoyevsky and Tolstoy.'[1] Except that they are not religious writers but 'philosophers', in the broader French sense of the term, we could also add Georg Christoph Lichtenberg and Otto Weininger. He was not widely read in either English or French literature, though von Wright assimilates his work to Pascal's. He was more sensitive to music than to any other form of art and Schubert was his favourite composer.

Wittgenstein was still in Cambridge late in 1940, when I was sent there on an army course, but he left soon afterwards to become a medical orderly at Guy's Hospital in London, and later rose to be an assistant at a Clinical Research Laboratory in Newcastle-upon-Tyne. In neither case did he let it be known that he was a university professor. He returned to Cambridge in the autumn of 1944.

From the start Wittgenstein appears to have disliked being a professor. In a letter to Malcolm written in the summer of 1945 he speaks of the business of being a professor of philosophy as 'an absurd job' and 'a kind of living death'.[2] Nevertheless he took his duties seriously. Malcolm, who returned to Cambridge in 1946, reports that Wittgenstein had added a two-hour weekly at home to his pair of two-hour weekly classes, besides spending separate afternoons with Elizabeth Anscombe, W.A. Hijab and Malcolm himself. Wittgenstein also thought it his duty to attend the weekly evening meetings of the Moral Science Club. I know from my own experience that when he was there

---

[1] Malcolm and von Wright, op. cit., p. 21.
[2] ibid., p. 43.

he dominated the discussion and that no one ventured to contradict him. This was one of the reasons why Broad disliked him and thought him a bad influence.

By the summer of 1947 Wittgenstein had decided to resign his professorship. He took advantage of the fact that he was entitled to a term's leave and spent the autumn in Austria. On his return to Cambridge, he submitted his resignation which became effective at the end of the year. He was succeeded by von Wright, whose reign was also short. He and his wife quite soon decided that they would prefer to make their home in their native Finland and in 1951 the Cambridge Chair passed into the eminently capable hands of John Wisdom.

After resigning his professorship, Wittgenstein at once went to live in Ireland, first on a farm at Wicklow, and then in a seaside hut in Galway, where he stayed in solitude for at least six months. The local fishermen are said to have been impressed by his skill in taming birds. Then, after paying short visits to Austria and to Cambridge, he settled for several months in a hotel in Dublin, where he found himself able to do philosophical work.

Malcolm, who had in the meantime become a professor at Cornell, in New York State, had for a long time been pressing Wittgenstein to visit him and Wittgenstein finally accepted, making the sea-crossing in July 1949 and staying in America until October. On the whole he appears to have enjoyed his stay, taking part in discussions with Malcolm and other philosophers at Cornell. In one respect he was an easy guest. I quote from Malcolm's Memoir: 'My wife once gave him some Swiss cheese and rye bread for lunch, which he greatly liked. Thereafter he would more or less insist on eating bread and cheese at all meals, largely ignoring the various dishes that my wife prepared. Wittgenstein declared that it did not much matter to him *what* he ate, so long as it was always the *same*.'[1] He was also a handyman about the house.

Towards the end of his stay with the Malcolms, Wittgenstein's health gave way and this made him anxious to return to Europe. The doctors at Cambridge diagnosed his illness as cancer of the prostate but assured him that his life was not in imminent danger. He spent the spring of 1950 in Vienna, beginning to compile the notes which

[1] ibid., p. 85.

were collected and published by his executors in 1969 under the title of *On Certainty* with the German text and an English translation as usual on facing pages. I find it the most lucid of all Wittgenstein's works. He returned to England in April 1950 and except for a short visit to Norway in the autumn lived at Oxford in Elizabeth Anscombe's house until February 1951. He was invited to give the John Locke Lectures at Oxford but refused. He had read a paper to the Oxford Philosophical Society on Descartes's *Cogito* in 1947, with H.A. Prichard as his chief antagonist, and the meeting had not been an unqualified success. But Wittgenstein's reason for declining the John Locke invitation was just that he did not feel capable of giving formal lectures to a large audience. It should however be added that he also wrote to Malcolm that Oxford was 'a philosophical desert'.[1]

By the spring of 1951 Wittgenstein's health had grown worse and he returned to Cambridge. He had a horror of being left to die in hospital and his doctor, Dr Bevan, took him into his own house. He continued to work on the question of certainty and that of colour concepts and he went out for walks, often with Mrs Bevan who had overcome her original fear of him. After one of these walks on 27 April he fell violently ill and two days later he was dead.

In his *Portraits from Memory* Russell tells the following story of Wittgenstein as a young man: 'He used to come to my rooms at midnight, and for hours he would walk backwards and forwards like a caged tiger. On arrival, he would announce that when he left my rooms he would commit suicide. So, in spite of getting sleepy, I did not like to turn him out. On one such evening after an hour or two of dead silence, I said to him, "Wittgenstein, are you thinking about logic or about your sins?" "Both," he said, and then reverted to silence.'[2]

I believe this story to be characteristic of Wittgenstein's personality. His engagement in philosophy, or indeed in whatever else he undertook, was serious and unrelenting. He judged human beings harshly, not least himself. Even so, his last words were: 'Tell them I've had a wonderful life.'[3]

[1] Malcolm and von Wright, op. cit., p. 98.
[2] p. 27.
[3] Malcolm and von Wright, op. cit., p. 100.

2

THE *TRACTATUS*

As I remarked in my book *Philosophy in the Twentieth Century*,[1] it looks as if the main theses of the *Tractatus* can be very easily summarized. The world is said to be a totality of facts which themselves consist in the existence of what in the original German are called '*Sachverhalten*', translated by Ogden as 'atomic facts' and perhaps more felicitously by Pears and McGuinness as 'states of affairs'. The states of affairs are composed of simple objects, each of which can be named. These names can be significantly combined in ways that express elementary propositions. Each elementary proposition is logically independent of all its fellows. They are all positive and each of them depicts a possible state of affairs which consitutes its sense. These pictures themselves are facts and share a logical and pictorial form with what they represent. Their possession of this form is something that is not assertible but merely shown. The fact that they are logically independent means that in order to give a complete account of reality one has to say which of them are true and which of them are false. In other words, reality consists of the respective existence and non-existence of all possible states of affairs. There is no need to add the rider that this list of possibilities is exhaustive; this emerges from the fact that no other attempts to depict states of affairs will be well formed.

Not all significant propositions are elementary. There are also compound propositions, which are formed out of elementary propositions by the repeated use of the logical operator of double negation, neither-nor. This operator, like the other 'logical constants' of simple negation, disjunction, conjunction and implication, which are all definable in terms of it, does not stand for any object. Its use serves

[1] pp. 111-12.

17

merely to distribute truth and falsehood among the elementary propositions on which it operates. The result is that all significant propositions, which are not themselves elementary, become what is tech-
nically known as truth-functions of elementary propositions. There are
two limiting cases. A proposition may be in conflict with all the elementary truth-distributions, in which case it is a contradiction, or it
may agree with them all, in which case it is a tautology. The true
propositions of logic are all tautologies, in this sense. One might expect
the same to be said of the true propositions of pure mathematics, but
Wittgenstein, for all his respect for Frege and Russell, does not acquiesce in their 'reduction' of mathematics to logic. He prefers to
characterize the mathematical propositions as equations. They are not,
however, represented as differing from logical tautologies in any important fashion. They serve a similar purpose in that they facilitate the
drawing of deductive inferences, but they also share with logical tautologies the failure to say anything about the world. Saying something
about the world is the perquisite of elementary propositions and of the
compound propositions which discriminate among their distributions
of truth.

If a series of signs fails to express either an elementary proposition
or a compound proposition, in the foregoing sense, and also does not
serve either to affirm or deny a mathematical equation, then it does
not express any proposition at all. In short, it is nonsensical. According
to Wittgenstein, 'most of the propositions to be found in philosophical
works are not false but nonsensical'. They are said 'to belong to the
same class as the question whether the good is more or less identical
than the beautiful'.[1] In one of the concluding paragraphs of the
Tractatus[2] the term 'metaphysical' is employed to characterize these
peccant utterances of philosophy and it came to be used in this pejorative way by those, like the members of the Vienna Circle and others,
including myself, who adopted Wittgenstein's stance on this matter.

Whether Wittgenstein's own use of the term was always pejorative
is not clear. It would be if he restricted its application to the product
of philosophical attempts to compete with or supplant the natural
sciences, but not if he took it to cover all the cases in which an attempt

[1] *Tractatus*, 4.003.
[2] ibid., 6.53.

was made to say what, on his principles, could not significantly be said. These cases included ethical, aesthetic and religious discourse, of a kind that did not meet his stipulations, but also had an importance in his eyes which he would not have attached to such gibberish as 'the good is more identical than the beautiful'. There is a tension in his thought which is displayed in his asserting both that the propositions of natural science set a limit to what can be said and that 'we feel that even when *all possible* scientific questions have been answered, the problems of life remain completely untouched'.[1] There is a similar ambivalence in his conception of philosophy. He consistently distinguishes it from the natural sciences and treats it as an activity rather than a body of doctrine. At one point it is said to be 'a critique of language'[2] and, as such, it is supposed to result in 'the clarification of propositions', 'to set limits to what cannot be thought by working outwards through what can be thought' and 'to signify what cannot be said by presenting clearly what can be said'.[3] This might be thought to be a fair description of the enterprise of the *Tractatus* itself and indeed Wittgenstein, having anticipated in the preface to his book the proposition with which he ends it, made famous in the Ogden rendering 'Whereof one cannot speak, thereof one must be silent',[4] goes on to say that the *truth* of the thoughts which the book advances seems to him definitive and unassailable.

Notoriously, however, the penultimate paragraph of the book runs: 'My propositions serve as elucidations in the following way: anyone who understands them eventually recognizes them as nonsensical, when he has used them – as steps – to climb up beyond them (He must, so to speak, throw away the ladder after he has climbed up it). He must transcend these propositions, and then he will see the world aright.'[5]

The conception of philosophy as a critique of language seems also to have been discarded. For in the previous paragraph we are told: 'The correct method in philosophy would really be the following: to say nothing except what can be said, i.e. propositions of natural sci-

---

[1] ibid., 6.52.
[2] ibid., 4.0031.
[3] ibid., 4.112–4.115.
[4] ibid., 7.
[5] ibid., 6.54.

ence – i.e. something that has nothing to do with philosophy – and then, whenever someone else wanted to say something metaphysical, to demonstrate to him that he had failed to give a meaning to certain signs in his propositions. Although it would not be satisfying to the other person – he would not have the feeling that we were teaching him philosophy – *this* method would be the only strictly correct one.'[1]

This is indeed consistent with Wittgenstein's dismissal of his own philosophical utterances as nonsensical, though one can hardly fail to sympathize with the would-be philosopher who feels that he has been put upon a very meagre diet. What is quite unacceptable is that one and the same series of pronouncements should be both devoid of sense and unassailably true. I shall return to this point later on.

I said earlier that the main argument of the *Tractatus* was easily summarized. So, indeed, it is, but the summary conceals many difficulties. They start with the conception of elementary propositions. Wittgenstein thought that it fell within the province of logic to show that there must be such things, but not to say what they were. That was a matter for what he called the application of logic,[2] which must surely be an empirical procedure even though understanding logic is said not to be.[3] He gives no indication, however, how this quest is to be conducted and the remarks that he makes about elementary propositions, and the simple objects which they are supposed to depict, are not only abstruse but ill-equipped to yield a coherent theory. It is to be remembered that Wittgenstein was not, as Russell mistakenly suggested in his introduction, attempting to sketch the lineaments of an ideal language, but claiming to probe to the roots of the language that we actually use.

Let us begin then by asking why there have to be elementary propositions. The answer is that they are needed to depict the primitive states of affairs which are formed by the combination of simple objects. But why do there have to be simple objects? The answer given in the *Tractatus* runs from proposition 2.02 to proposition 2.0212. 'Objects are simple. Every statement about complexes can be resolved into a statement about their constituents and into the propositions that describe the complexes completely. Objects make up the substance of the

---

[1] *Tractatus*, 6.53.
[2] ibid., 5.557.
[3] ibid., 5.552.

world. That is why they cannot be composite. If the world had no substance, then whether a proposition had sense would depend upon whether another proposition was true. In that case we could not sketch out any picture of the world (true or false).' This chain of reasoning is not very easy to follow, but light is thrown on it by one of the *Philosophical Remarks*, a book for which Wittgenstein wrote a preface in November 1930 but which he never went on to publish.[1] Edited by Rush Rhees it appeared in German in 1964 and in an English translation only in 1975. In the course of its thirty-sixth paragraph we are told: 'What I once called "objects", simples, were simply what I could refer to without running the risk of their possible non-existence; i.e. that for which there is neither existence nor non-existence and this means: what we can speak about *no matter what may be the case*.'

The notion of there being things 'for which there is neither existence nor non-existence' is puzzling, but I take it to be no more than a clumsy way of reformulating the preceding condition that the objects should be such as to afford us security of reference: and this means either that they are properties, for which it is required only that the predicates standing for them be intelligible, or, if they are individuals, that they are capable of being named and not merely described. If they could only be described, the attempt to refer to them would run the risk of failure. It happens that just one person answers to the description 'the wife of G.E. Moore' and nothing answers to the description 'the wife of Ludwig Wittgenstein' but both descriptions make equally good sense.

But is it true of anything that it can only be described? If an individual satisfies a description which carries with it the implication of existence, then surely it can also be named. This is so, and it shows that we are still missing the point of Wittgenstein's argument. The contrast between names and descriptions on which he is relying must be that, while what is named may also be describable, it is only the use of a name, as opposed to a description, that can guarantee the existence of what is being referred to. Then the simplicity of an object consists in its being namable in this fashion.

This brings us round in a circle, but it does not bring us home. For it is just not true of ordinary proper names that their use guarantees the existence of the objects to which they are intended to refer. Neither

[1] See p. 7 above and p. 34 below.

am I thinking only of the use of names in what is avowedly legend, mythology or fiction. I happen to believe that the legend of King Arthur is based upon fact, but whether I am right on this point or not my statement that King Arthur fought the Saxons makes equally good sense.

It was for this reason that Russell came to think that the only genuine names were what he called logically proper names, which he equated with demonstratives, and since the intention to point to a physical object might always be frustrated by one's undergoing an illusion, he took these demonstratives to denote the contents of present sense-experience which he and Moore called sense-data. For my own part, I believe that the introduction of sense-data serves a useful purpose in the analysis of perception, but I see no need for the recourse to names which are guaranteed to succeed in their reference. The fact that they happen to succeed should be enough. The view which I am attributing to Wittgenstein that without such infallible names 'we could not sketch out any picture of the world (true or false)' seems to be simply false, and indeed there is a passage in which he appears to acknowledge this, at least by implication. 'A proposition', he says, 'that mentions a complex will not be nonsensical, if the complex does not exist, but simply false.'[1]

In any case the simplicity of sense-data is not enough to fit them for the role of Wittgenstein's simple objects. For like Hume's 'impressions', sense-data are 'perishable and fleeting' whereas Wittgenstein's objects, charged, as we have seen, with making up the substance of the world, are said to be 'unalterable and subsistent'; it is just their configuration that is 'changing and unstable'[2] and it is the changing and unstable configurations of these objects that produce states of affairs.[3]

But where are these unalterable and subsistent objects to be found? I rule out scientific particles, partly because the law of the conservation of energy, which anyhow is not a logical truth, does not prevent them individually from being perishable and fleeting, partly because I cannot consider them as susceptible of being named, most of all, perhaps, because I cannot see how the repeated operation of double negation,

[1] *Tractatus*, 3.24.
[2] ibid., 2.0271.
[3] ibid., 2.0272.

applied to propositions which depict the configuration of atoms, could possibly yield the propositions of our everyday discourse. And indeed, Wittgenstein himself says in the passage which I quoted from his *Remarks* that 'the visual table is not composed of electrons'.

If, as we must, we discard the assumption that only simple objects can be named, we allow room for the suggestion that states of affairs consist of perceptible qualities on the model of Locke's simple ideas, united by a relation of compresence. This would obliterate the common distinction between names and predicates, but it would appear that Wittgenstein has already done so by his insistence that his primitive sentences consist only of names. Possible states of affairs would then consist of all the admissible complexes of simple qualities including their actual combinations. Apart from the difficulty, which is common to all interpretations, of finding a plausible criterion of simplicity, the two main obstacles to this view are that Wittgenstein employs Russell's symbolism in which different types of letters are used to designate particular objects and their properties and, more seriously, that he rejects the identity of indiscernibles. 'Russell's definition of " = " is inadequate', he says, 'because according to it we cannot say that two objects have all their properties in common (Even if this proposition is never correct, it still has *sense*).'[1]

I see no way of overcoming this last difficulty except by adding regions of space and stretches of time to our list of objects. If these were identified by systems of co-ordinates, then attaching sense to the denial of the identity of indiscernibles would mean allowing the possibility of a duplication of this system of co-ordinates with the same distribution of perceptual qualities, as in a mirror universe or one of eternal recurrence. Such possibilities are indeed far-fetched but it seems to me that they anyhow have to be admitted if the identity of indiscernibles is not to be treated as a necessary truth.

In favour of the position which we have now reached is Wittgenstein's saying in the *Tractatus* that 'space, time and colour (being coloured) are forms of objects'.[2] It is true that this succeeds, at a fairly short distance, the maddening remark that 'In a manner of speaking, objects are colourless',[3] but what I take this to mean is that objects as

[1] ibid., 5.5302.
[2] ibid., 2.0251.
[3] ibid., 2.0232.

such do not have any determinate degree of colour, or whatever other perceptual quality is in question. The qualities must, however, be instantiated in some determinate degree. In this way we can also make some sense of proposition 2.0321, in the Ogden translation which here seems to me more faithful to the original German: 'The substance of the world *can* only determine a form and not any material properties. For these are first presented by the propositions – first formed by the configuration of objects.' It will be seen that I am taking material properties to be determinate and more hazardously taking the configuration of objects to embrace the spatio-temporal location of determinable qualities.

Another advantage of this interpretation is that it requires numbers to be included in elementary propositions, as measuring both the spatio-temporal co-ordinates and the degrees of such perceptual qualities as admit gradation, a point on which Wittgenstein insisted in his paper on 'Logical Form', a paper which looks back to the *Tractatus*, even though Wittgenstein is said to have thought poorly of it. What we cannot accommodate are propositions 2.061 and 2.062 of the *Tractatus*: 'States of affairs are independent of one another. From the existence or non-existence of one state of affairs it is impossible to infer the existence or non-existence of another.' For it would not be possible for two different colours, or different shades of colour, wholly to occupy the same place at the same time and this would also apply to other sense-modalities. Wittgenstein had acknowledged this point in the *Tractatus*[1] but tacitly shrugged it aside. He had come to take it seriously by the time he wrote the paper on 'Logical Form' and accordingly excluded the joint truth of two such competitive propositions from his table of truth-distributions. He derived such exclusions from what he called the grammar of colour and the like, and thereby avoided the admission of natural necessity.

The rejection of natural necessity, at least as regards science, is well supported by the stretch of the *Tractatus* running from proposition 6.3 to proposition 6.372, a train of argument for which the physicist Heinrich Hertz deserves more acknowledgement than the passing mention that he receives. The law of causality is said to be not a law but the form of a law. Newtonian mechanics is felicitously compared with a

---

[1] *Tractatus*, 6.3751.

net which is thrown over phenomena, and the possibility is allowed of the use of nets with different meshes to describe the world. Laws like the principle of sufficient reason are said to be about the net and not about what the net describes. We are told that the procedure of induction consists in accepting as true the *simplest* law that can be reconciled with our experiences, and that this procedure has no logical but only a psychological justification. Where I disagree with Wittgenstein is in his finally castigating the view that the laws of nature explain natural phenomena as an illusion. For what would count as giving an explanation if uncovering these laws does not?

Perhaps the fact that the elementary propositions are likely to contain numbers warrants our according them the same multiplicity as the states of affairs which they designate, and perhaps this could be taken as a sufficient reason for speaking of them as pictures. In the main, however, it seems to me that the use that Wittgenstein makes of the pictorial metaphor is a source of more darkness than light. It obscures the fact that physical likeness acquires a symbolic function only when it is chosen as a method of representation. In particular, since it is only one out of many possible methods of representation, it does not serve to explain in what representation consists.

I am also unable to accept Wittgenstein's theory of probability. He says quite correctly that propositions are neither probable nor improbable in themselves, since an event either occurs or it does not,[1] but combines this with the mistake of treating statements of probability as elliptical and *a priori*. 'If', he says, 'T_r is the number of the truth-grounds of a proposition "r" and if T_{rs} is the number of the truth-grounds of a proposition "s" that are at the same time truth-grounds of "r" then we call the ratio $T_{rs} : T_r$ the degree of *probability* that the proposition "r" gives to the proposition "s".'[2] The fatal objection to any 'logical' theory of this sort is that it makes no allowance for the weight of evidence. All estimates of probability emerge from the theory as equally valid, provided that the ratios have been correctly calculated, no matter how slender the evidence. Our practice of trying to acquire a greater quantity and a greater variety of evidence as a basis

---

[1] ibid., 5.153.
[2] ibid., 5.15.

for our judgements of what is likely to happen can find no foothold in Wittgenstein's theory of probability.

An objection which has been brought against the system of the *Tractatus*, but may not be fatal to it, is that it makes no provision for unfulfilled conditionals. As we have seen, Wittgenstein adopts Russell's interpretation of logical operators, whereby the formula 'if p, then q' is treated as equivalent to 'not-p or q', with the consequence that it is sufficient for the truth of a conditional that its antecedent is false. But, as has often been remarked, it is undesirable to have to assent to any possible result of an experiment, just so long as the experiment is not actually carried out. Even so, I think it just possible to defend Wittgenstein's position on the ground that it does not commit him to the denial of the existence of any actual state of affairs. Unfulfilled conditionals, of the awkward sort, would be assigned not to the domain of fact but to the secondary domain of what the American pragmatist C.S. Peirce called the arrangement of facts. They would then be adjudged not true or false, but acceptable or unacceptable according as they fitted or failed to fit into whatever arrangement was in favour. I tried to develop a theory of this type in the third part of my book *Probability and Evidence* but cannot claim to have made it watertight. It is rather contrary to the spirit of the *Tractatus* but, as we shall see, accords somewhat better with Wittgenstein's later views.

An objection, which Wittgenstein explicitly recognizes, to his view that compound propositions merely serve to distribute truth and falsehood among elementary propositions is the appearance of propositions in psychology of such forms as 'A believes that *p* is the case' or 'A has the thought that *p*'. For he admits that 'if these are considered superficially, it looks as if the proposition *p* stood in some kind of relation to an object A'.[1] And he adds that Russell, Moore and others have construed such propositions in this way.

Wittgenstein's rebuttal of this view is not easy to understand. 'It is clear', he says, 'that "A believes that *p*", "A has the thought that *p*", and "A says *p*" are of the form " '*p*' says p": and this does not involve a correlation of a fact with an object, but rather the correlation of facts by means of the correlation of their objects.'[2] And he adds, even

[1] *Tractatus*, 5.541.
[2] ibid., 5.5421.

more mysteriously, 'This shows too that there is no such thing as the soul – the subject, etc – as it is conceived in the superficial psychology of the present day. Indeed a composite soul would no longer be a soul.'[1]

I am indebted for my interpretation of this difficult passage to Mr Brian McGuinness. He has suggested to me that when Wittgenstein wrote of the form ' "p" says p', he intended the p within quotation marks to stand for a propositional sign and the p which it was said to say as the thought which the sign expressed. The person 'A' to whom reference was ostensibly made in the unanalysed proposition would then be 'reduced' in Humean fashion to a series of thoughts.

The most valiant attempt to uphold such a theory of the self was made by William James and for reasons which I set out at length in my book *The Origins of Pragmatism* I do not think that he succeeded, my main objection being that he could not make provision for the persistence of personal identity through the gaps that occur in consciousness. Nevertheless all that this shows is that a theory of the sort that James advocated needs to be supplemented by an appeal to bodily continuity, and it leaves it open for Wittgenstein to admit propositions only as the meanings of signs the embodiments of which occur in such a fortified series. Unfortunately, the theory of representation which is set out in the *Tractatus* leaves it uncertain whether propositions of the form ' "p" says p' can be fitted into this scheme.

When Wittgenstein says that there is no such thing as the soul, the subject, etc, as currently conceived, and adds that a composite soul would no longer be one, he may be expressing his dissatisfaction with theories of the Jamesian type. But it is more likely that he is looking forward to a later section of the book, the section beginning with the proposition 5.6: '*The limits of my language* mean the limits of my world' and ending with the proposition 5.641: 'Thus there really is a sense in which philosophy can talk about the self in a non-psychological way. What brings the self into philosophy is the fact that "the world is my world". The philosophical self is not the human being, not the human body, or the human soul, with which psychology deals, but rather the metaphysical subject, the limit of the world – not a part of it –.' In between, come the celebrated remarks that 'What the

[1] ibid., 5.5421.

27

solipsist is getting at (*meint*) is quite correct: only it cannot be *said*, but makes itself manifest' that 'there is no such thing as the subject that thinks or entertains ideas', that 'nothing *in the visual field* allows you to infer that it is seen by an eye' and that 'solipsism, when its implications are followed out strictly, coincides with pure realism. The self of solipsism shrinks to a point without extension, and there remains the reality co-ordinated with it.'

What are we to make of all this? It is now well established that Wittgenstein inherited these ideas from Schopenhauer, to the extent of clothing them in very much the same words, and that Schopenhauer obtained his notion of the metaphysical self, the transcendental ego, from Kant. Unfortunately, tracing Wittgenstein's oracular sayings to their source is not sufficient to explain them. Nor does the authority behind them entitle us to take them on trust. Authority comes down also on the other side. So far as William James could see, 'Transcendentalism is only Substantialism grown shame-faced and the Ego only "a cheap and nasty" edition of the soul. All our reasons for preferring the "Thought" to the "Soul" apply with redoubled force when the Soul is shrunk to this estate.... The Ego is simply *nothing*: as ineffectual and windy an abortion as Philosophy can show.'[1]

I do not seek to disguise the fact that my sympathy lies with William James, but this does not absolve me from the task of trying to find reasons for what Wittgenstein says. I think that his dicta appear in the most favourable light if we relate them to Kant's insight that intuitions without concepts are blind. In other words, all visions of the world are mediated through some conceptual system, and it is logically inevitable that the conceptual system in which the world is delivered to me should be my own. Not only that but it is equally inevitable that the experiences which finally sustain or nullify my beliefs should be my own experiences, themselves conforming with my system of interpretation. It is in this sense that the world is my world, and in so far as my system of concepts is clothed in language, it also becomes a truism that the limits of my language mean the limits of my world.

This is not, however, to deny that the world contains other persons, or that their conceptual systems may coincide with mine. There is

---

[1] *The Principles of Psychology*, vol. 1, p. 365.

indeed a philosophical problem about one's justification for attributing consciousness to others and, in particular, for crediting them with experiences which parallel one's own. This is a problem which continued to exercise Wittgenstein and it is one to which I shall return. All that I wish to say now is that solipsism is not the answer. I do not believe that I am the only conscious being in the world and if anyone else claims to be so I know from my own experience that he is mistaken. What tempts philosophers is a sort of generalized solipsism but I shall show later on that this is incoherent.

Not only does my world contain other persons, it also contains myself, my body and its movements, my thoughts and feelings and sensations. Nor do I occupy a privileged position in it, except as an authority concerning my own experiences. It existed for many years before I was born and I do not doubt that it will continue to exist for many years after I am dead. To say that 'there is no such thing as the subject that thinks or entertains ideas' is literally false, unless it is intended to deny the uniqueness of the subject. There are many such subjects of whom I am one.

I suspect that where Wittgenstein goes astray is in his endorsement of Schopenhauer's simile of the eye and the visual field. It is just not true that my world stands in need of a self outside it by which it is manufactured in the way that my visual field needs an organ outside it by means of which it can be seen. The conceptual scheme which I bring to bear on the world is supplied to me within the world with my acquisition of language and if I were to change it, as the result, say, of some new scientific discovery, this would again be a spatio-temporal event. Nor is the failure of a person's attempt to capture himself because, as Ryle put it, 'his quarry was the hunter'[1] anything to the purpose. One thought reflects upon another and the fact that this activity can, at any rate in theory, proceed through an indefinite number of stages, gives us no warrant for postulating anything 'beyond' the everyday empirical self.

So how does solipsism coincide with pure realism? If it is the result of the shrinkage of 'the self of solipsism', by which Wittgenstein must surely here be taken to intend the metaphysical self, to a point without extension, then this self has shrunk to nothing, just as James took it

---

[1] *The Concept of Mind*, p. 198.

to be all along. And being nothing, it performs no function. We are not to submit to the sleight of hand by which it is overtly abolished and then tacitly re-instated as an imperial agent, a Pooh-Bah of which nothing can be said.

I said earlier on that Wittgenstein could not have it both ways. It cannot be the case both that his assertions are true and that they are devoid of sense. Russell makes this point in his introduction to the *Tractatus* and so does F.P. Ramsey in one of his Last Papers. 'Philosophy', he there says, 'must be of some use and we must take it seriously; it must clear our thoughts and so our actions. Or else it is a disposition we have to check, and an inquiry to see that this is so; i.e. the chief proposition of philosophy is that philosophy is nonsense. And again, we must then take seriously that it is nonsense and not pretend, as Wittgenstein does, that it is important nonsense!'[1] Ramsey's famous quip 'But what we can't say we can't say, and we can't whistle it either', was not explicitly directed against Wittgenstein, as is widely supposed, but was a comment on the suggestion that general propositions be treated as infinite conjunctions, with the result that we are forced to have 'a theory of conjunctions which we cannot express for lack of symbolic power'.[2] It is true, however, that Wittgenstein appears to furnish a target for this special criticism, with his view that generality appears only at the level of elementary propositions, *all* of which he surely quite unwarrantably takes to be 'given'.

There is, indeed, no denying that Wittgenstein believed, throughout his philosophical career, that philosophers were easily led into talking nonsense and that the principal function of philosophy, as he conceived and practised it, was to uncover and dismantle the linguistic traps into which they fell. This did not commit him to holding that the remarks about language which he made to serve this end were themselves nonsensical, and I cannot recall a passage in his later works in which he suggests that they were. In the case of the *Tractatus* we have to choose between his dismissal of its contents as senseless and his claim that they were true, and I prefer to believe that he thought them true.

Nevertheless, it has now become clear that, in one central respect,

---

[1] *The Foundations of Mathematics*, p. 263.
[2] ibid., p. 238.

the outlook of the *Tractatus* was misunderstood by the members of
the Vienna Circle and the young English philosophers, including myself, who were strongly influenced by it. Even if we decline to take
Ramsey's derisive phrase 'important nonsense' as representing what
Wittgenstein genuinely thought of the *Tractatus* itself, it does represent
his estimate of what he saw as lying beyond the limits of language.
We took it for granted that he judged metaphysics to be worthless,
whereas in so far as he equated it with what he called 'the mystical',
and included in it judgements of value and the appreciation of the
meaning of life, his attitude was much more akin to that of Kant
whose criticisms of metaphysics were intended to limit the scope of
the understanding in the interests of faith. This comes out very strongly
in a letter quoted in Paul Engelmann's *Letters from Ludwig
Wittgenstein*[1] and quoted again by Bryan Magee in his revelation of
Wittgenstein's debt to Schopenhauer.[2] 'My work', wrote Wittgenstein,
'consists of two parts: the one presented here plus all that I have *not*
written. And it is precisely this second part that is the important one.
My book draws limits to the sphere of the ethical from the inside as
it were, and I am convinced that this is the ONLY *rigorous* way of
drawing those limits. In short, I believe that where many others to-day
are just *gassing*, I have managed in my book to put everything firmly
into place by being silent about it.'

There are, indeed, indications of this verdict in the text of the
Tractatus, as when it is said that 'The solution of the riddle of life in
space and time lies *outside* space and time',[3] or '*How* things are in the
world is a matter of complete indifference for what is higher. God
does not reveal himself *in* the world',[4] or 'We feel that even when *all
possible* scientific questions have been answered, the problems of life
remain completely untouched. Of course there are then no questions
left, and this itself is the answer';[5] most of all perhaps in the preface
where, after claiming that he has finally solved all the problems with
which his book deals, Wittgenstein goes on to say that, if that is so,
'the second thing in which the value of this work consists is that it

---

[1] p. 143.
[2] B. Magee, *Schopenhauer*, p. 293.
[3] *Tractatus*, 6.4312.
[4] ibid., 6.432.
[5] ibid., 6.52.

shows how little is achieved when these problems are solved'. These hints were not lost on Otto Neurath, the most tough-minded member of the Vienna Circle, whose comment on Wittgenstein's conclusion 'Whereof one cannot speak, thereof one must be silent' was 'One must indeed be silent, but not *about* anything.'

Here I confess that my sympathies lie with Neurath. This is not to deny the occurrence of mystical experiences, or yet to deny that those who do enjoy them are entitled to set a great value on them. What I want to reject is the suggestion that they reveal the existence of any-thing 'higher', or that they supply an answer to 'the problems of life' which is beyond the reach of science. Nor am I content just to bury ethics and aesthetics in 'the mystical'. It is true that I am still attracted to the 'emotive' theory of ethics which I put forward in *Language, Truth and Logic*, at a time when I was under the spell of the *Tractatus* and still more of the Vienna Circle, and that the emotive theory does exclude purely ethical statements from the domain of statements of fact. At the same time it does attempt to give an explanation of their meaning. Neither was this the only type of theory that the positivism of the Circle could accommodate. Its leader, Moritz Schlick, treated the questions of ethics, in a book with that title, as purely naturalistic, depending on the nature of human desires and the ways in which they could be satisfied.

In this context it is interesting to take note of a lecture on 'Ethics' which Wittgenstein delivered to a society in Cambridge either in the autumn of 1929 or some time in 1930. The manuscript was preserved and published in the *Philosophical Review* in January 1965. Wittgen-stein quickly passes by the most common use of words like 'good' or 'bad' to indicate success or failure in the attainment of some pre-established standard, or 'right' or 'wrong' as an estimate of the method of achieving some pre-determined end, in order to try to explain what he means by such expressions as 'absolute good' or 'absolute value'. And at this point he thinks he can do no more than draw the attention of his audience to three sorts of experience. The first is the experience of wonder at there being anything at all, of which Wittgenstein says that he believes it to be what people were referring to when they said that God had created the world; the second is the experience of feeling absolutely safe, which some would describe as the experience of feeling safe in the hands of God; and the third is the experience of feeling guilty which one might try to describe by saying that God disapproves of our conduct.

It is noteworthy that all these experiences have a religious flavour; yet Wittgenstein does not make them the basis for an argument that there is a God. On the contrary, this conclusion falls into his container of important nonsense. One need only quote the conclusion of his lecture: 'My whole tendency and I believe the tendency of all men who ever tried to talk about Ethics or Religion was to run against the boundaries of language. This running against the walls of our cage is perfectly, absolutely hopeless. Ethics so far as it springs from the desire to say something about the ultimate meaning of life, the absolute good, the absolute valuable, can be no science. What it says does not add to our knowledge in any sense. But it is a document of a tendency in the human mind which I personally cannot help respecting deeply and I would not for my life ridicule it.'

An interesting point is that the experiences to which Wittgenstein turns to throw light on his sense of absolute values do not provide the basis for any set of moral principles. They offer no guidance for the conduct of life. Yet there is abundant evidence that Wittgenstein maintained very strong moral attitudes and that his judgements of people's conduct, including his own, were frequently harsh. So far as I know, he never attempted to bring them into accord with any philosophical theory.

My account of the *Tractatus* has been chiefly critical and we shall see that Wittgenstein himself came to reject its main approach. Nevertheless, it retains an important position in the history of philosophy. Its truth may not be unassailable and its very great influence partly due to a misunderstanding, but among the productions of this century it continues to stand out for its beauty and its power.

3

THE PERIOD OF TRANSITION

The years following Wittgenstein's return to Cambridge were for him a period of intense philosophical activity. Apart from the article on 'Logical Form' which he allowed to appear in the *Supplementary Proceedings of the Aristotelian Society* for 1929, he published none of this work in progress, but he preserved a vast quantity of notes, a number of which he arranged in various patterns, and his literary executors have been fanatically diligent in ordering and preparing them for public consumption. The most coherent of the books that have resulted is the one entitled *Philosophische Bemerkungen* in the German edition, which, as I have said, Rush Rhees edited and published in 1964. In the English translation by Raymond Hargreaves and Roger White which appeared in 1975 under the title *Philosophical Remarks*, it runs to just under 350 pages. The text is mainly taken from the typescript which Wittgenstein submitted to Bertrand Russell in 1930, as requested by the Council of Trinity College. We have seen that Russell's report was favourable[1] but it appears to have been based more on conversations with Wittgenstein than on a study of the work of which Russell reported to the Council that he had read about a third. I think it unlikely that he read the manuscript all the way through before returning it to Moore who kept it for Wittgenstein. That Wittgenstein had serious thoughts of publishing it is shown by the existence of a preface dated November 1930. The book is there said to be written for such men as are in sympathy with its spirit, one which seeks to grasp the world at its centre, in opposition to the current fashion of building larger and more complicated structures. Wittgenstein adds that he would like to say 'This book is written to the glory of God', but for the current

[1] See above, pp. 7 and 21.

likelihood that such a statement would be misunderstood. What he means by it, he then says, is that 'the book is written in good will'.

In the book, as we now have it, there are two appendices, the first consisting partly of a score of notes on the difference in the proper use of the words 'complex' and 'fact' and partly of a short disquisition on the concept of infinity in mathematics, the second taken from Friedrich Waismann's shorthand transcript of conversations with Wittgenstein in Vienna between December 1929 and September 1931. It runs to about thirty pages and is mainly devoted to the philosophy of mathematics, with Wittgenstein querying the need for a proof of the consistency of a mathematical system, on the ground that contradictions can always be dealt with as they arise. The two items in the first of the appendices are both assigned to the year 1931.

An even longer work which runs to nearly 500 pages in its English version is the one entitled *Philosophische Grammatik*, which Rush Rhees edited and published in 1969.[1] The English translation by Anthony Kenny appeared in 1974. Rush Rhees's edition is almost entirely based on a typescript which Wittgenstein completed in 1933 and revised in 1934, drawing on manuscripts which he had written in the years 1930 to 1932. It is divided into two almost equal parts, the first and slightly longer being given the English title 'The Proposition and Its Sense' and the second 'On Logic and Mathematics'. To a very considerable extent, it supplies us with slightly different versions of themes which appear also in *Philosophical Remarks* and material which is set out in a more orderly fashion in *The Blue Book*.

Wittgenstein's indefatigable literary executors also brought out in 1967 a set of jottings which he had put together in a file. They gave these their German title *Zettel* and published them in the same format as the *Tractatus* with the German text and its English translation by Miss Anscombe on facing pages. Most of these scraps are assigned by the editors, Anscombe and von Wright, to the years 1945-8, but a few are said to go back as far as 1929.

Overlapping with *The Brown Book* is a series of three notebooks for Lectures on 'Private Experience' and 'Sense-data', of which their editor, Rush Rhees, assigns the first to the end of 1934 or the beginning of 1935 and the third to March 1936. These notes were published in

[1] See above, p. 7.

35

a number of *The Philosophical Review* which came out in 1968. They are mainly in English with occasional recourse to German. They were worth printing, not only as marking a stage in Wittgenstein's progress towards the stance that he adopted in his *Philosophical Investigations*, but as having a certain interest in their own right.

The *Philosophical Remarks* are of particular interest because they display the closest co-incidence of Wittgenstein's views with those of the Vienna Circle. In particular, he commits himself at various places to a strong version of the principle of verifiability. Thus, we find him saying that 'the meaning of a question is the method of answering it',[1] that 'every proposition is a signpost for a verification',[2] that 'the verification is not *one* token of the truth, it is *the* sense of the proposition. (Einstein: How a magnitude is measured is what it is)',[3] that 'to understand the sense of a proposition means to know how the issue of its truth or falsity is to be decided'[4] and that 'a proposition has sense only if I know what is the case if it is false'.[5] This last quotation calls to mind the principle of falsifiability which Karl Popper advanced, as he thought, in opposition to the Vienna Circle, but there remains the difference that Popper intended his principle to serve as the hallmark of scientific statements, not as a general criterion of meaning.

A serious doubt concerning the principle of verifiability is whether the sense of a proposition is tied to the actual or hypothetical outcome of its verification by the best-placed observer, or whether we make it depend on the capacities of its interpreter, taking into account his identity and the spatio-temporal position that he occupies. The objection to the first course is that the concept of the best-placed observer is hopelessly imprecise. The objection to the second course is that it leads to a counter-intuitive rendering of the sense of propositions about the past, or the experiences of other persons, and indeed that the only sentences which have a definite meaning for anyone are those that record or predict his present or future experiences. The objections to the second course seem the more serious; nevertheless, that is the one

[1] *Philosophical Remarks*, para. 27.
[2] ibid., 150.
[3] ibid., 166.
[4] ibid., 43.
[5] ibid., 154.

that Wittgenstein adopts. To show how far he allows this to take him, I am going to quote the whole of his lengthy fifty-sixth remark:

Anyone wishing to contest the proposition that only the present experience is real (which is just as wrong as to maintain it) will perhaps ask whether then a proposition like 'Julius Caesar crossed the Alps' merely describes my present mental state which is occupied with the matter. And of course the answer is: no, it describes an event which we believe happened ca. 2,000 years ago. That is, if the word 'describes' is construed in the same way as in the sentence 'The proposition "I am writing" *describes* what I am at present doing'. The name Julius Caesar designates a person. But what does all that amount to? I seem to be fighting shy of the genuinely philosophical answer! Propositions dealing with people, i.e. containing proper names, can be verified in very different ways. – We still might find Caesar's corpse; that this is thinkable is directly connected with the sense of the proposition about Caesar. But also that a manuscript might be found from which it emerged that such a man never lived and that the accounts of his existence were concocted for particular purposes. Propositions about Julius Caesar must, therefore, have a sense of a sort that covers this possibility. If I utter the proposition: I can see a red patch crossing a green one, the possibilities provided for in 'Julius Caesar crossed the Alps' are not present here, and to that extent I can say that the proposition about Caesar has its sense in a more indirect way than this one.

Everything which, if it occurred, would legitimately confirm a belief, determines logically the nature of this belief. That is, it shows something about the logical nature of the belief.

The proposition about Julius Caesar is simply a framework (like that about any other person) that admits of widely differing verifications, although not all those it would allow in speaking of other people – of living people, for instance.

Isn't all that I mean: between the proposition and its verification there is no go-between negotiating this verification?

Even our ordinary language has of course to provide for all cases of uncertainty, and if we have any philosophical objection to it, this can only be because in certain cases it gives rise to misinterpretations.

One misinterpretation of which I was guilty in my *Language, Truth and Logic* emerged in my proposal to give a mentalistic account of one's own experiences and a behaviouristic account of the experiences of others. It was only some time later that I realized that this proposal was incoherent. The reason why it was incoherent is that if one is obliged by one's criterion of meaning to interpret the experiences of another person behaviouristically, one cannot attach any sense to the hypothesis that he himself interprets them mentalistically. I concluded that there could be no asymmetry in the analysis of a proposition about a person's experiences, whether the proposition was expressed by others or by the person himself. It followed either that one must accept a behaviouristic account of one's own experiences or else somehow manage to justify the extension of a mentalistic interpretation to the experiences of others. It has always seemed to me that a fatal objection to the first course is, in the felicitous phrase of C.K. Ogden and I.A. Richards in their *The Meaning of Meaning*, that it obliges one to feign anaesthesia. The difficulties attached to the second course are notorious but I have long refused to consider them insuperable. The position which I now hold was suggested to me by Professor Hilary Putnam in an article on 'Other Minds' which he contributed to *Logic and Art*, a collection of essays in honour of Nelson Goodman. As I put it in my book *The Central Questions of Philosophy*:

> My attributing consciousness to others is not just a matter of my accepting, on the strength of a doubtful analogy, the generalization that two different series of events, one mental and one physical, habitually go together. It is a consequence rather of my accepting a whole body of theory which enables me to account for the behaviour of others by crediting them with conscious thoughts and sensations and emotions and purposes. My ability to entertain this body of theory does depend on my having learned from my own experiences what these mental states are like, but my justification for accepting it is that it has been found, in Putnam's words, to have 'genuine explanatory power'.[1]

I do not know what comment Wittgenstein would have made on this passage, had it been written earlier and come to his notice. I am

---

[1] op. cit., pp. 134-5.

pretty sure that he would have taken exception to the temper of its approach. We shall see that the problems arising from what has been called the egocentric predicament occupied him very largely throughout the remainder of his career. Notoriously, he campaigned against the possibility of there being private languages, but exactly what he had in mind, how close it brought him to behaviourism, what his arguments were, how they were related to other theses that he held and whether they prove what he intended, are all questions which I shall later be examining in detail.

In the concluding passages of his remarks Wittgenstein makes one of his rare incursions into the philosophy of science. It is of interest that he adopts the principle of verifiability in a very strong form and applies it ruthlessly. Again, a long quotation will be the best way of showing how far he is prepared to go. The following extract forms the greater part of remark 225 and the beginning of 226:

> All that's required for our propositions [about reality] to have a sense, is that our experience *in some sense or other* either tends to agree with them or tends not to agree with them. That is, immediate experience needs only confirm something about them, *some* facet of them. And in fact this image is taken straight from reality, since we say 'There's a chair here', when we only see *one* side of it.
>
> According to my principle, two assumptions must be identical in sense if every possible experience that confirms the one confirms the other too. Thus, if no empirical way of deciding between them is conceivable.
>
> A proposition construed in such a way that it can be uncheckably true or false is completely detached from reality and no longer functions as a proposition.
>
> The views of modern physicists (Eddington) tally with mine completely, when they say that the signs in their equations no longer have 'meanings' and that physics cannot attain to such meanings but must stay put at the signs. But they don't see that these signs have meaning in as much as – and only in as much as – immediately observable phenomena (such as points of light) do or do not correspond to them.
>
> A phenomenon isn't a symptom of something else; it is the reality.

A phenomenon isn't a symptom of something else which alone makes the proposition true or false: it itself is what verifies the proposition.

An hypothesis is a logical structure. That is, a symbol for which certain rules of representation hold.

The point of talking of sense-data and immediate experience is that we're after a description that has nothing hypothetical in it. If an hypothesis can't be definitively verified, it can't be verified at all, and there's no truth or falsity for it.

The interpretation of these seemingly downright remarks is not unproblematic. For instance, what are the phenomena that constitute reality? In the light of the last item that I quoted, it is tempting to equate them with sense-data, on the ground that propositions, which alone are about reality, must be either true or false, that it is not considered possible for them to be true or false unless they can be definitively verified, and that they can be definitively verified only if they refer to present or future sense-data. The question is whether this interpretation can be made to fit Wittgenstein's examples. It might be squeezed into covering phenomena such as the points of light to which the signs that occur in scientific theories are said to owe their meaning, if the appropriate sense-data are conceived, like Russell's sensibilia, as being available to any observer who is in the proper position to obtain them, but what of the example of the chair? The existence of the chair is affirmed in a proposition, which has to be true or false, but here there is no question of the proposition's being definitively verified, unless definitive verification comes down to nothing more than some degree of confirmation in immediate experience. This, however, appears to be ruled out by Wittgenstein's saying shortly afterwards, 'When people say, by the proposition "There's a chair here", I don't merely mean what is shown me by immediate experience, but something over that, you can only reply: whatever you can mean must connect with some sort of experience, and whatever you *can* mean is unassailable'.[1] Yet it is not clear why the proposition about the chair should be regarded as less of a 'framework' than the proposition about Julius Caesar, except that it is couched in the present tense. I do not think that we should attach any weight to the fact that a proper name

[1] *Remarks*, 230.

is employed in the one case and not in the other. After all, if we were disposed to be whimsical we could bestow a proper name on the chair and conversely Caesar could be identified by a description not even containing another proper name, for example as the one and only man who was killed by receiving so many stab wounds at such and such a place and date.

The use of the word 'proposition' in the example of Julius Caesar seems inconsistent with the requirement that propositions be definitively verified and with the assumption, which Wittgenstein appears to make, that a necessary condition for satisfying this requirement is that the proposition be expressed by a sentence in the present or the future tense. Perhaps this was a slip and Wittgenstein on further reflection would have classified this and other historical statements as hypotheses. This is the line that I took in *Language, Truth and Logic*, but it may well have accorded more with Schlick's usage than with Wittgenstein's. It may also be the case that Wittgenstein's usage fluctuated. On the one hand he was inclined to bring objects like Julius Caesar and the chair, however the references to them were dated, down to the level of phenomena, which alone were real, as opposed to the mere signs that figured in Eddington's equations. On the other hand, he was inclined to treat any assertion about the past, no less than the ingredients of physical theories, as fulfilling the conditions which he regarded as essential for a hypothesis, that it not be definitively verifiable but that 'it arouses an expectation by admitting of future confirmation'.[1] So far as I can discover, he never adopted the phenomenalist thesis that physical theories can be translated into the set of propositions describing the observable states of affairs that would confirm them; for one thing he declared that the confirmation of a hypothesis is never completed.[2] In the same set of remarks he characterized a hypothesis as 'a law for forming propositions' or alternatively as 'a law for forming expectations'. I think he can most fairly be said to have treated the experiences which would fulfil these expectations as constituting the 'cash-value' of the hypothesis. 'Cash-value' is a term employed for this purpose by William James, a

[1] ibid., 228.
[2] ibid.

philosopher whom I believe that Wittgenstein respected. At any rate, his dicta of this period fit easily into the pragmatist tradition.

I was gratified to discover that in the concluding passages of his *Philosophical Remarks* Wittgenstein gives up the logical theory of probability which he had sketched in the *Tractatus*. I have already stated my objections to this view and two quotations will suffice to show, not indeed that Wittgenstein had anticipated them, but that he had arrived at the same conclusions, possibly by a different route. 'It always looks', he says, 'as if our experience (say in the case of card shuffling) agreed with the probability calculated *a priori*. But that is nonsense. If the experience agrees with the computation, that means my computation is justified by the experience, and of course it isn't its *a priori* element which is justified, but its bases, which are *a posteriori*. But those must be certain natural laws which I take as the basis for my calculation, and it is those that are confirmed, not the calculation of the probability.'[1] And later he says, 'When a gambler or an insurance company is guided by probability, they aren't guided by the probability calculus, since we can't be guided by this on its own, because *anything* that happens can be reconciled with it: no, the insurance company is guided by a frequency actually observed. And that of course is an absolute frequency.'[2] It is, I must add, an absolute frequency only in the sense that it has a definite statistical value. There is no guarantee that the ratio will be preserved in future instances.

The pragmatic tenor of Wittgenstein's thinking at this period is again in evidence in the early part of *The Blue Book*. We are advised at the outset to substitute for the question 'What is the meaning of a word?', the question 'What is an explanation of the meaning of a word?' or 'What does the explanation of a word look like?' One immediate benefit of this change of approach is that it diminishes the temptation to think of meanings as a special category of objects, or that of being satisfied with any general set of answers conforming to the pattern of the assertion that predicates stand for properties. Wittgenstein sees that the fundamental problem is that of explaining how a series of noises or written marks acquires what he calls a life. His

[1] *Remarks*, 232.
[2] ibid., 234.

own general answer is that 'if we had to name anything as the life of the sign, we should have to say that it was its use'.[1]

The slogan 'Don't ask for the meaning, ask for the use', as John Wisdom has expressed it,[2] became very popular among analytical philosophers, but it was never made clear how it was intended to supplement 'The meaning of a statement is its method of verification', except for its making provision for the fact, on which Wittgenstein increasingly laid stress, that there are many uses of sentences besides the purely assertory. Neither does Wittgenstein proceed to clarify it in *The Blue Book*, or at least not in any straightforward fashion. He tells us that 'the sign (the sentence) gets its significance from the system of signs, from the language to which it belongs',[3] but does not enlarge on this. Instead he exposes a series of errors into which philosophers, and perhaps not only philosophers, are apt to fall when they are confronted with the question of the nature of signs.

The first of these mistakes, which Gilbert Ryle also brought to light in *The Concept of Mind*, is to suppose that what makes a series of marks or noises, let us say a sentence, significant is its having some accompaniment. This accompaniment is usually taken to be some mental process. But the objections to this are first that we constantly use words meaningfully, especially in conversation, without being aware of the occurrence of any mental duplicates, and secondly and decisively that such mental processes, which may, though they need not, accompany our utterances, and may indeed occur on their own, themselves consist in the employment of signs. On this point I think there should be no disputing that Wittgenstein and Ryle are right.

Let us then allow ourselves to say, with Wittgenstein, that thinking is essentially the activity of operating with signs. In the case where the thought is expressed in writing we can say that the activity is performed by the hand; where the activity consists in speaking we can say that it is performed by the mouth and larynx; but what of the cases in which the thought is given no overt expression? In these cases we are tempted to say that the activity is performed by the mind, and there we go astray if we forget or fail to realize that we are resorting to a metaphor. The mind is not an agent in the same sense as the hand.

[1] *The Blue Book*, p. 4.
[2] See his *Logic and Discovery*, p. 87.
[3] *The Blue Book*, p. 5.

But why should we not say that we think with our brains? Surely the brain plays a causal role in our thinking just as our hand does in our writing and the mouth and larynx in our speaking? The answer, which does not appear to me of very great importance, is that there is a difference in the links of the causal chain. The brain also plays a causal role in our writing or speaking, but when our thinking does not consist in the overt use of signs, there is no intermediate factor in their production such as the hand or the tongue. It occurs to me also that we are inclined to assimilate the hand and tongue to instruments like pens or telephones, whereas we lack this inclination in the case of the brain. One reason may be that we think of our muscles and the organs of speech as subject to our wills in a way that our brains are not. Yet when we decide to embark upon a course of thinking, the consequent processes in our brains result from the exercise of our wills, whatever this consists in, and conversely many bodily movements take place without being consciously willed.

Wittgenstein sets the problem in a different light by offering an explanation of our tendency to treat the head or the brain as the locality of thought. He makes the rather questionable claim that 'if ... we talk about the locality where thinking takes place we have a right to say that this locality is the paper on which we write or the mouth which speaks'.[1] And then he adds that 'if we talk of the head or brain as the locality of thought, this is using the expression "locality of thinking" in a different sense'.[2] I agree that the sense is different from that in which the paper might be said to be the locality of the thoughts that I write down, but not that it is markedly different from the sense in which the thoughts that I speak are located in my mouth. As I remarked a little earlier, this is merely a matter of picking out different stages in a causal chain.

This causal explanation is too simple for Wittgenstein, who ascribes our inclination to locate thoughts in our head to our forming too literal a conception of thinking as an activity on a par with writing and speaking. He also suggests that our awareness of the possibility of expressing the same thought in different languages leads us to distinguish a thought from the various sentences which embody it, and to

[1] *The Blue Book*, p. 7.
[2] ibid.

look for a place for it just as the written tokens of the sentences have their places, and in a less straightforward way the utterances of the spoken sentences also. Eventually he comes round to the causal explanation, envisaging an elaborate experiment in which the thinker simultaneously, perhaps by means of a mirror, inspects his own brain. Many contemporary philosophers would say that the subject was observing one and the same series of events, from the inside and the outside, but Wittgenstein, to my mind rightly, says that speaking in this way 'does not remove the difficulty', which is presumably that of pin-pointing the thought. He prefers to say that the subject is observing a correlation of two phenomena, one that of seeing his brain work, and the other which he is more likely to call the thought, one that 'may consist of a train of images, organic sensations, or on the other hand of a train of the various, tactual and muscular experiences which he has in writing or speaking a sentence'.[1] Wittgenstein would prefer to see the question 'Where is thought itself?' rejected as nonsensical, but relents so far as to admit the expression 'the thought takes place in the head' as a causal hypothesis deriving its meaning from one aspect of his fanciful experiment.

A very common mistake against which Wittgenstein puts us on our guard is that of supposing that in order to recognize an object or a property we need to compare it with a sample. Since, in most cases, no physical sample will be available, the sample is believed to be a mental image. The objections to this assumption take the same form as those that were fatal to the view that written or spoken sentences acquire their meaning from inner accompaniments. In the first place we constantly recognize familiar things or properties without the aid of any images, and secondly and decisively the resort to images does nothing to explain recognition, for if it is to be of any use the image must itself be recognized. Wittgenstein brings this point out very neatly by adverting to the case where one invites someone to imagine a yellow patch. 'Would you still', he asks, 'be inclined to assume that he first imagines a yellow patch, just *understanding* my order, and then imagines a yellow patch to match the first?'[2] The point of this example is not to show that images never play a part in our acts of recognition,

[1] ibid., p. 8.
[2] ibid., p. 12.

but to make it obvious that their contribution is not necessary. Perhaps Wittgenstein exaggerates a little when he goes on to say that this illustrates the method of philosophy, since not all philosophy consists in dispelling illusions of this sort, but it is a good illustration of his own practice at its best.

Wittgenstein reviews in some detail what he calls the grammar of such expressions as 'to wish', 'to expect', 'to long for'. He suggests that in the case where 'I wish so and so to happen' is the description of a conscious process, it is improper to ask the speaker whether he knows what he wishes. He is entitled to brush the question aside. But the reason for this, as Wittgenstein sees it, is not that one has an infallible acquaintance with one's present states of consciousness, but that our language makes no provision for the expression of doubt in such a case. Rather than say 'Of course, I know what I wish', one should say 'Of course, there is no doubt', meaning by this that here it makes no sense to talk of there being any doubt. 'In this way', Wittgenstein concludes, 'the answer "Of course I know what I wish" can be interpreted as a grammatical statement.'[1] It seems to me, on the contrary, that it makes perfectly good sense to speak of a person's not knowing what he wishes or even of his being mistaken on this point. One might ask what would show him to be mistaken and the answer would lie in his behaviour, for instance in his failing to take an easy opportunity of fulfilling the wish. Admittedly, there is the escape route of saying that his wish was very evanescent, but I do not see that grammar obliges us to take it.

Such phenomena as wishing and expecting or, most importantly, believing may all miss their mark and so give rise to what Wittgenstein calls a beautiful example of a philosophical question: How can one think what is not the case? As he puts it: 'If I think that King's College is on fire when it is not on fire, the fact of its being on fire does not exist. Then how can I think it? How can we hang a thief who doesn't exist? Our answer can be put in this form: I can't hang him when he doesn't exist; but I can look for him when he doesn't exist.'[2]

One might believe that there was no more to be said but Wittgenstein, like a water-diviner, detects a philosophical trap. He supposes

---

[1] *The Blue Book*, p. 30.
[2] ibid., p. 31.

us to be misled by the terms 'object of thought' and 'fact' and by what he counts as the different meanings of the word 'exist'. He even counts himself as having succumbed to this confusion when he equated facts in the *Tractatus* with complexes of objects. What he is putting in question is the assumption that imaginary objects must have real components, fictively assembled. An obvious example is a centaur who is pictured as combining the hindquarters of a horse with the head and arms and torso of a man: no doubt we can also imagine colours to be combined in ways that are not actually exhibited. On the other hand, when our imagination transposes primary colours, surely we must already be acquainted with actual instances of them. This is a version of Hume's principle that our 'ideas' copy previous impressions, but even Hume admitted a possible counter-example, allowing our imagination the power to fill a gap in a range of shades which have been presented to our sight. Wittgenstein prefers to make the point that the dependence of our power to imagine colours upon our visual perceptions, even to the extent that it exists, is not a logical necessity.

Another disposition which he reprobates is that of our introducing dummies as objects of thought, in cases where our beliefs being false, or our wishes unsatisfied, they cannot be said to be directed upon facts. As instances of such dummies he cites the senses which are ascribed to sentences, where these senses are presented as objects, or the propositions which sentences are said to express. Wittgenstein calls these interlopers shadows of facts. There is indeed no harm in talking of senses, in this usage, or of propositions as a convenient way of registering the fact that sentences in different languages, or different sentences in the same language, may be equivalent in meaning. We go astray only if we suppose that manoeuvres of this sort have any explanatory value, or mistake the shadows for substantial entities.

Towards the end of *The Blue Book* Wittgenstein reverts to the problem of the egocentric predicament. He presents the solipsist as asking 'How *can* we believe that the other has pain; what does it mean to believe this? How can the expression of such a supposition make sense?'[1] and then remarks of the common-sense philosopher who finds 'no difficulty in the idea of supposing, thinking, imagining that some-

[1] ibid., p. 48.

one else has what I have' that he 'does not solve but skips the difficulties which his adversaries see, though they too don't succeed in solving them.'[1] Wittgenstein attaches great importance to distinguishing what he calls the metaphysical proposition 'I can't feel his pain' from the experiential proposition. 'We can't have (haven't as a rule) pains in another person's tooth',[2] and he shows his habitual ingenuity in devising situations in which we should find it natural to say that a person feels pain in another person's body or even in an inanimate object like a table. It would be a matter of where he points when asked to locate the pain and how the pain is assuaged. The purpose of these extravagant examples is to show that the philosopher who entangles himself in the premiss that he has direct access, as he puts it, only to his own experiences is not drawing attention to any matter of fact. Even in the strange circumstances of his feeling pain in his neighbour's tooth, he would not say that he felt his neighbour's pain. But this means that he makes it what Wittgenstein calls a rule of grammar that one person does not feel another's pain; he treats the feeling of another's pain not as a factual but as a logical impossibility.

Wittgenstein goes on to say that 'if we exclude "I have his toothache" from our language, we thereby also exclude "I have (or feel) *my* toothache".'[3] This is unobjectionable if it means no more than that the word 'my' is redundant in this instance, but there are indications that this is not all that Wittgenstein means to imply. For instance he claims a little later on that 'To say "I have pain" is no more a statement *about* a particular person than moaning is.'[4] This seems to me simply false. It is possible that Wittgenstein was led astray here by his choice of an example. There is some plausibility in treating the utterance of the words 'I am in pain' as an expression of pain like moaning or wincing, but nothing of this sort applies to the general run of statements about one's current thoughts and feelings. It does not apply to 'I am thinking about tomorrow's game', 'I can just smell the daffodils from here', 'I remember having my pocket picked in the Métro' and a host of other examples. Perhaps more pertinently it does not apply to 'My tooth has stopped aching' or 'I shall be in pain when the dentist

[1] *The Blue Book*, p. 48.
[2] ibid.
[3] ibid., p. 55.
[4] ibid., p. 67.

goes to work on me tomorrow'. There seems no reason why the change to the present tense should make such a vast difference to the analysis.

I believe that Wittgenstein is wrong also to object to people's saying that they know that they are in pain. His reason is that it would make no sense to say 'I know that I am in pain' unless it also made sense to say 'I don't know whether I am in pain' and that this second condition is not satisfied. I find this unconvincing on two counts. In the first place, it is not obvious to me that to speak of 'being in pain without knowing it' is a deviant expression. I think it could apply to animals and infants and even to human adults who had been corrupted by Christian Science or had unwarranted faith in the power of a pain-killing drug. But even if I were mistaken on this point, I should still wish to say that it is a very common occurrence for someone to know that he is in pain. All that is required is that he honestly assents to the statement that he is in pain, that the statement be true and that his acceptance of it be causally based on the occurrence of the feeling; and surely all three of these conditions are frequently satisfied. I choose to speak of the patient's honestly assenting to the statement that he is in pain rather than his believing it, to avoid having to quibble over the question whether it is proper to speak of believing, in cases where there is no serious doubt. At this point I wish to reserve discussion of my view that knowledge entails belief.

It is possible that Wittgenstein is being ironical when he suggests that the attraction of solipsism, the temptation to say that only what one sees oneself is *really* seen, is nourished on grammar, as if what the solipsist demanded were that we change our way of speaking, so that whereas others are said to have experiences, without any special emphasis, only he is said really to have them, or that when we talk of there being experiences, without assigning an owner to them, it is to be understood that they are his. It is obvious that such concessions would not and should not satisfy him. As I pointed out earlier, the mistake into which philosophers are tempted to fall is that of trying to generalize solipsism, which is not at all the same thing as claiming a special position only for oneself.

If grammar comes into it at all, it is only at the point where our genuine regret that other people are opaque, that we are not so well aware of their thoughts and feelings as we should wish to be, arrives at the stage of our chafing at the logical impossibility of our merging our separate identities: and even then it is not plain that a change of notation would be of any use. All the same I agree that the slide from the empirical to the logical does contribute some of its acuity to the problem of Other Minds. John Wisdom, who does indeed acknowledge a debt to Wittgenstein, brings this out particularly well in his series of articles entitled 'Other Minds' which he contributed to *Mind* throughout the war and published in 1952 as a book.

Wittgenstein's notes for Lectures on 'Private Experience' and 'Sense-data' are mainly a distillation of remarks made in *The Blue Book* together with some anticipations of the positions for which he was to argue in the *Philosophical Investigations*. He says much that I consider to be false, as when he claims that my saying that when I ascribe toothache to another person I am supposing that he has what I have when I have toothache entirely misrepresents the use of the word 'toothache'; or that we should have no use for words like 'seeing red' if their application were severed from the criteria of behaviour; or that I cannot be justified in using a sentence to record my present experiences 'just by what is now the case'; or that talk of private experience is a degenerate construction of our grammar; or that I cannot be said to know indirectly what another person is feeling unless I can also be said to know it directly. But I postpone discussion of these questionable assertions until I come to examine the *Investigations*, in which their grounds and consequences are set out in more detail.

4

THE BROWN BOOK

The date of *The Brown Book*, 1934-5, allies it with what I have called the period of transition in Wittgenstein's thought, but the extent to which it is preparatory to the *Investigations* makes it worth singling out for special attention. As I have said, it consists of a text, with numbered paragraphs, dictated to two of his pupils in English. We are told in an introduction by Rush Rhees that Wittgenstein made a German version of the greater part of it, presumably with a view to publication, but abandoned it five-sixths of the way through, with the comment, emphatically written in German, equivalent to 'This whole attempt at a revision, from the start right up to this point, is *worthless*'. It is not easy to understand why Wittgenstein was so dissatisfied with this work as opposed, say, to the *Investigations*, the bulk of which he seriously considered publishing. Admittedly, the train of thought in *The Brown Book* is not easy to follow, but neither is it in the *Investigations*. Perhaps one has the more oppressive feeling of being nagged in going through *The Brown Book*, but it is only a difference of degree. The *Investigations* is more ambitious and contains the more brilliant images, but *The Brown Book* is just as incisive in the points that it succeeds in making.

As it is presented to us, *The Brown Book* is divided into two parts, the first covering fifty and the second almost sixty pages. The main topic of the first part is that of what Wittgenstein called language-games; the second part is a commentary on a number of concepts such as those of recognizing, willing, remembering and understanding.

Mention of language-games had already been made in *The Blue Book*, but there they seem to be presented as simplifications of certain aspects of a language like our own. In *The Brown Book*, they are put forward not, in Wittgenstein's own words, 'as incomplete parts of a language, but as languages complete in themselves, as complete systems of human communication'.[1] Nevertheless they are very much simpler than natural languages like German or English and they are surely intended to throw light on some features of such natural languages. They are not so intrinsically fascinating that there would otherwise be any point in making them up.

The first language which we are asked to imagine is one that serves for communication between a builder and his mate. The mate has access to building materials, consisting of cubes, bricks, slabs, beams and columns, and the language consists of the words 'cube', 'brick', 'slab' and 'column'. When the builder calls out 'brick' his mate fetches him a brick; when the builder calls out 'slab' his mate fetches him a slab, and so forth. Since nothing is made of the fact that the word 'beam' is missing from the list, this may be an oversight on Wittgenstein's part. It could however be a reminder that this is an exceptionally poor language, even if its only purpose is to serve the building trade. Wittgenstein asks us to imagine a society in which this is the only system of language and speaks of a child's being trained to use it in the same sense as animals are trained to come to heel, or beg, or whatever it may be. 'Part of the training', Wittgenstein says, 'is that we point to a building stone, direct the attention of the child towards it, and pronounce a word' and he adds 'I will call this procedure *demonstrative* teaching of words'.[2] Though Wittgenstein does not say so, he surely intends this to be a model of the way children, learning their first natural language, are taught the use of many common nouns.

Since the language-games in *The Brown Book* are supposed to be autonomous, it is surprising to find Wittgenstein digressing to consider the objection that the word 'brick' in the language he has just described does not have the same meaning as it has in 'our language'. He remarks that in suitable contexts the utterance of the word 'brick' could for an English speaker mean what is meant by 'fetch me a brick' and argues that the speaker who uses the single word need not have the longer sentence 'in mind'. He cites William James as speaking of 'specific feelings accompanying the use of such words as "and", "if", "or",[3]

[1] *The Blue and Brown Books*, p. 81.
[2] ibid., p. 77.
[3] ibid., p. 78.

and allows that certain gestures are often connected with such words, and that visual and muscular sensations are connected with these gestures. He adds, however, that sensations of the kind in question do not always accompany the use of such words, so that we should be wrong in identifying the sensations with their meaning. 'If', he says, 'in some language the word "but" meant what "not" means in English, it is clear that we should not compare the meanings of these two words by comparing the sensations which they produce.'[1]

Wittgenstein's second language-game is an extension of the first. The builder's mate is now supposed to have learned by heart the series of numerals from one to ten. In the first game he obeyed his master's orders silently but this time when he hears, for example, the words 'five slabs' he pronounces the numerals from one to five, takes up a slab on the occasion of each utterance, and carries the collection of slabs to the builder. He has been taught the use of the ten numerals demonstratively, the method being that of showing him groups of objects of the same shape and uttering the appropriate numeral, so that he hears the word 'three' when he is shown a group of three bricks or three slabs, 'six' when he is shown a group of six bricks or six cubes and so forth. Wittgenstein comments, again surprisingly, that his having the builder's mate learn the series of numerals by heart introduces a new feature to which nothing corresponds in the first game. One must therefore assume that in the first game the builder's utterances simply acted as stimuli which evoked automatic responses. Perhaps that was the point of comparing the mate's training to that of an animal. Nevertheless the practice of ostensive teaching would appear to occur in both cases. Wittgenstein admits that the pronouncing of certain words together with a gesture is a common feature, but maintains that there is a difference in the way the gesture is used. 'The difference', he says, 'is blurred if one says "In one case we point to a shape, in the other to a number".'[2] We have to take his word for this, since he goes on to say that it is only when we look at the example of a language completely worked out in detail that the difference becomes obvious and clear. Here he seems to be reverting to his earlier notion

[1] ibid., p. 79.
[2] ibid.

of language-games as fragments of natural languages, rather than languages which are complete in their own right.

The third game introduces what Wittgenstein calls 'a new instrument of communication', the use of a proper name. The builder pronounces the name of a particular brick, or whatever, and his mate fetches that particular object. Wittgenstein declares that the demonstrative teaching of a proper name differs from the demonstrative teaching of the use of a common noun or from that of the use of a numeral but he does not explain how they differ. All he says is that 'this difference does not lie in the act of pointing and pronouncing the word or in any mental act (meaning?) accompanying it'.[1] This would appear to leave as the only possible source of difference, a difference in the objects which provide the pointing with its target, but Wittgenstein rejects this also. His argument is that even though a man who points, e.g. to a blue jersey, knows and can tell us whether he is pointing to the colour or pointing to the shape, these two intentions are not distinguished by characteristic mental acts. How then are they to be distinguished? Wittgenstein, again forgetting that his language-games are supposed to be complete in themselves, gives the unhelpful answer that the difference 'does not lie in the act of demonstration, but rather in the surrounding of that act in the use of the language'.[2] Perhaps the idea is that the reference is elicited by further questions, which implies that the speaker at any rate knows what he intends. This leaves us with the puzzle how he knows, if it is not in virtue of any mental act.

A regrettable omission from this language-game is any provision for the use of a proper name in the absence of the object which it purports to denote. Once the use of the name has been taught, the fact that the man has to go and look for the object in question may be of no practical account: he finds and fetches it. On the other hand, it may make a very serious difference: that particular brick, let us say, has been destroyed. And here the important point is not so much that the builder's mate can no longer play his part in the game, as that the builder can still play his. His order has not lost or changed its meaning.

It was because a situation of this sort can always obtain in the case

[1] *The Blue and Brown Books*, p. 80.
[2] ibid.

of what are ordinarily counted as proper names that Russell thought that the 'real proper names', as Wittgenstein puts it, were words like 'there', 'here', 'now', 'this'. Wittgenstein alludes to this view of Russell's, saying that Russell took such words to refer to the individuals which analysis would show to be the ultimate constituents of reality, but fails to explain how Russell was led to this conclusion. He himself introduces the word 'there' into the fourth of the language-games, its function being to indicate the place where the man has put the slab that he has fetched. Once more, surprisingly, Wittgenstein says that the answer to the question whether the use of the word 'there' is taught demonstratively in this language is Yes and No. The ground for this equivocation is that we should hesitate to say that the word 'there' names a place. Ordinarily, indeed, such words are not counted as proper names, presumably because of the constant shifts in their references, but there is surely no doubt that their use is taught demonstratively.

Wittgenstein devises more than a score of language-games which it would be tedious to go through in detail. Written signs are introduced, as well as pictures and samples. The point, already made in *The Blue Book*, is again stressed, that recognition and comparison may but need not, even in the absence of physical samples, depend on the assistance of mental images. Various examples are given of training in the use of tables. If such a table consists of two columns of words and pictures, they would normally be read horizontally from left to right, the word pointing straight to the picture, but they could also be read criss-cross in various ways. The tables might be furnished with rules for reading them, like the instructions accompanying the pieces of a game, and those rules might be explained by further rules, but this process cannot continue indefinitely. At some point the learner may be allowed to have mastered the rules, without the need of any further directions. How this is shown and what it consists in are questions to which we shall find that Wittgenstein recurs.

For instance, at the end of the first part of *The Brown Book*, Wittgenstein proposes to study the use of the word 'reading' in order to elucidate the sense of being guided by a sign. He simplifies the question by not requiring that 'reading' should imply understanding what is read. He gives an account of what would entitle someone to qualify as a reading machine, and compares him with a beginner who spells out a few words, with someone who pretends to read but has merely memorized the text, and with the use of various means of translating Roman into Cyrillic script. The moral which he eventually draws is this:

> It was not the function of our examples to show us the essence of 'deriving', 'reading' and so forth through a veil of inessential features; the examples were not descriptions of an outside letting us guess at an inside which for some reason or other could not be shown in its nakedness. We are tempted to think that our examples are *indirect* means for producing a certain image or idea in a person's mind, – that they *hint* at something which they cannot show. This would be so in some such case as this: Suppose I wish to produce in someone a mental image of the inside of a particular eighteenth-century room which he is prevented from entering. I therefore adopt this method: I show him the house from the outside, pointing out the windows of the room in question, I further lead him into other rooms of the same period. –
>
> Our method is *purely descriptive*; the descriptions we give are not hints of explanations.[1]

At the beginning of the second part of *The Brown Book* Wittgenstein describes various circumstances in which we should say that someone recognized something as a pencil. In some cases where the subject has been taught the use of the word 'pencil' by being shown a paradigm, or by being given a description of the function of the object, he is said to attain the goal by a derivation, in others not. The question is raised whether the subject who had learned what a pencil was, experienced a feeling of familiarity on seeing the pencil after seeing other instruments which he could not identify, and the answer given is that what really might have happened is that 'he saw a pencil, smiled, felt relieved, and the name of the object came into his mind or mouth'.[2]

It is not very clear what the point of multiplying these examples is except to make us aware of their variety, perhaps yet again to disabuse us of the idea that recognition is marked by the presence of a distinctive mental act. Where a feeling of familiarity does obtain, Wittgen-

---

[1] *The Blue and Brown Books*, p. 125.
[2] ibid., p. 129.

stein suggests that it may consist in the feeling of relief which occurred in the circumstances of his last example.

In a discussion of the topic of similarity, much complicated by the fact, to which Wittgenstein hardly needs to call our attention, that 'we use the word "similar" in a huge family of cases',[1] he makes the helpful remark that it very often happens that 'the grammar of a word seems to suggest the "necessity" of a certain intermediary step, although in fact the word is used in cases where there is no such intermediary step. Thus we are inclined to say: "A man must understand an order before he obeys it", "He must know where his pain is before he can point to it", "He must know the tune before he can sing it" and such like.'[2] Are we to say then that understanding an order may consist in obeying it, that knowing where one's pain is may consist in pointing to it, that knowing the tune may consist in singing it? This hardly seems right, since it is obvious that one can understand an order without obeying it, that one can know where one's pain is and yet be prevented from pointing to it, that one can know a tune and yet be unable to sing it, for one or other reason such as the loss of one's voice. In every one of these cases a capacity extends beyond its actual exercise or even the power to exercise it on a particular occasion. It covers hypothetical as well as actual behaviour. All the same when the appropriate behaviour does take place, there may be nothing else on the scene to help make it a manifestation of the capacity in question. No doubt this was Wittgenstein's point. If so, it was yet another skirmish in his guerrilla warfare against mental acts.

These skirmishes multiply as the book proceeds. One of them concerns our use of the word 'to mean' in cases where we desire to clarify a rule or a reference. The question what constitutes following a rule, by which Wittgenstein was greatly preoccupied, is one that we shall be examining later on in detail, but we are provided here with a nice example of the use of the verb 'to mean' in the past tense to clarify a reference. Someone refers to Napoleon and is asked if he meant 'the victor of Austerlitz'. He replies quite truly that he did, even though when he spoke of Napoleon and predicated something else of him he most probably did not have the expression 'the victor of Austerlitz' in

[1] ibid., p. 133.
[2] ibid., p. 130.

mind. The proof that he meant the person so referred to just lies in this subsequent acceptance of the definite description.

It is characteristic of his position that, while admitting that a speaker's utterance of a sentence is not sufficient to show that he believes what he means it to express, Wittgenstein denies that there has to be something 'behind' the utterance and whatever gestures may accompany it, which is the real belief as opposed to the mere expression of it. He does not deny that there may be cases where the presence of a sensation of a special sort distinguishes meaning what one says from not meaning it, only that the distinction always takes this form. It may not be due to anything that occurs at the time of speaking but to various actions and experiences that occur before and after. Wittgenstein draws an analogy between the variety of factors that may constitute one's meaning or not meaning what one says, and the variety of features that may exhibit the distinction between a friendly and unfriendly face.

Here as elsewhere, Wittgenstein, in his propensity to identify thoughts and beliefs with their verbal or other physical expressions, passes over the very common cases where we keep them to ourselves. No doubt, like Ryle, he would frequently have been satisfied with a dispositional account, but apart from the difficulty of specifying the disposition, since there are many circumstances in which we should not say that the utterances of certain words evinced a belief in what they expressed, there would seem to be a great many cases of occurrent thoughts and even of occurrent beliefs which would remain to be accounted for. We might follow Ryle again in equating unspoken thoughts with silent soliloquies, and substitute silent assent to some form of words for occurrent but unavowed beliefs. The point of such manoeuvres in either case would be to ensure that these mental operations were embodied in the use of signs, whether or not this was openly manifested. The practice adopted by contemporary philosophers, like W.V. Quine, of rejecting what they call 'mental meaning' altogether, in favour of verbal behaviour, still strikes me as flying in the face of experience.

Towards the end of *The Brown Book* Wittgenstein invites us to consider various characteristics of voluntary and involuntary acts. In certain cases, obviously, there is a feeling of effort, as when one sets oneself to lift a heavy weight, but one can raise one's arm without any feeling of muscular strain and our action still be voluntary. Wittgenstein strangely suggests that in a large class of cases of this sort 'it is the peculiar impossibility of taking an observant attitude towards a certain action which characterizes it as a voluntary one'.[1] This seems to me just false. On the other hand I agree with Wittgenstein that it is a mistake to represent our volition as playing 'on a key-board of muscles, choosing which one it was going to use next'.[2] It is not even true in the case of voluntary action that we always know what we are going to do before we do it. Sometimes we do and sometimes we don't.

The moral to be drawn from this and countless other passages in *The Brown Book* is one that we shall encounter again in the *Investigations:* that the application of a word to a number of instances does not depend on their having a character, or set of characters, in common, but rather in their possession of a variety of features which constitute what Wittgenstein calls 'a family resemblance'.

[1] *The Blue and Brown Books*, p. 153.
[2] ibid.

5

THE FOUNDATIONS OF MATHEMATICS

A problem which greatly exercised Wittgenstein, after he resumed his interest in philosophy, was that of the status of the propositions of mathematics. There are references to it in the *Philosophical Remarks*, the *Philosophical Grammar* and most importantly, as we shall see, in the *Philosophical Investigations;* and a series of lectures which Wittgenstein gave in Cambridge on 'The Foundations of Mathematics' in 1939 was collected and published in 1976.

The main source, however, for Wittgenstein's ideas on this subject are to be found in a book entitled *Remarks on the Foundations of Mathematics*, assembled from his manuscripts by his literary executors, G.H. von Wright, Rush Rhees and Elizabeth Anscombe, translated by Anscombe, and published in 1956 with the German and English text on facing pages. The book is divided into five parts of which the first is assigned by the editors to the year 1937, with one contemporary appendix and one written in the period April 1938 to January 1939; the second part is assigned to the period October 1939 to April 1940, the third is taken from a manuscript of 1942, the fourth from two manuscripts of 1942 and 1943, and the fifth is held to have been written at various times but principally in 1941 and in the spring of 1944. The divisions are thus mainly chronological, but result in part from the editors' grouping of topics, in part from their notion of the development of Wittgenstein's views. I feel bound to say that this development is hard to trace. The *Remarks on the Foundations of Mathematics* is in my opinion the most difficult of the works that Wittgenstein's executors have so far compiled, and the one that has met with the least favourable reception, at any rate from logicians. Its outlook, however, is uniform. As always, in Wittgenstein's later work, the same themes keep recurring, the differences lying in the light in which they are presented. The remarks do not fit into any obvious sequence of composition.

The very title of the book is misleading, in so far as it may suggest that Wittgenstein was seeking a foundation for mathematics which would be an improvement on any that had so far been proposed. Frege and Russell had each endeavoured to reduce mathematics to logic, with the implication both that it would diminish any uncertainty that we might feel about the character of numbers and that it would provide a support for our mathematical beliefs. As we shall see, they had also felt their logical systems to be threatened by antinomies. Wittgenstein does not reject their programme on account of these antinomies, which we shall find him dismissing with remarkable insouciance. His position is rather that there is nothing to be gained by reducing mathematics to logic, however watertight the chosen system of logic might turn out to be. For the qualms which he feels about the necessary truth which is ascribed to mathematical propositions apply to the propositions of logic also.

In expressing these qualms Wittgenstein is unseating logic from the throne on which he had set it in the *Tractatus*. Almost the first question which comes up in the arrangement of his *Remarks on the Foundations of Mathematics* is the status of logical inference. Clearly this consists in the derivation of one proposition from another according to a rule, but what are we to take this to cover? If we are not in any way restricted, we can find some rule or other which will sanction any derivation that we please. But this is not what we are after. We want, as Wittgenstein puts it, 'to infer what really *follows*'. 'Is this', he continues, 'supposed to mean only what follows, going by the rules of inference, or is it supposed to mean: only what follows going by *such* rules of inference as somehow agree with some (sort of) reality? Here what is before our minds in a vague way is that this reality is something very abstract, very general, and very rigid. Logic is a kind of ultra-physics, the description of the "logical structure" of the world, which we perceive through a kind of ultra-experience (with the understanding e.g.).'[1]

The undermining of the status accorded to logic in the *Tractatus*

---

[1] *Remarks on the Foundations of Mathematics*, p. 6.

goes together with an abandonment of the search for ultimacy. 'What', we are now asked, 'does mathematics need a foundation for? It no more needs one, I believe,' says Wittgenstein, 'than propositions about physical objects – or about sense impressions, need an *analysis*. What mathematical propositions do stand in need of is a clarification of their grammar, just as do those other propositions.'[1]

Well, what is the grammar of a mathematical proposition? Or rather, what does Wittgenstein take it to be? There is no simple answer to either of these questions. I find it easier to start with the second of them, hoping that my attempt to extract and evaluate the answer to it will throw some light upon the first. What Wittgenstein principally sought to clarify was the concept of a mathematical rule, the character of mathematical proof, the importance attached to consistency in mathematics, the concept of an infinite series, the sense, if any, in which mathematical propositions are necessarily true, and the application of mathematics to experience.

Perhaps the single most important clue to Wittgenstein's approach is his saying that 'the mathematician is an inventor not a discoverer'.[2] This implies a rejection of the Platonic view of numbers as real abstract entities and, still more controversially, a rejection of the realistic view that a mathematical proposition must be true or false. An example to which Wittgenstein frequently resorts is that of the occurrence of a sequence of digits, for example the sequence 777, in the infinite expansion of pi, the ratio of the circumference of a circle to its diameter. Wittgenstein wants to say that unless we come across this sequence in the course of our calculation, the question has no answer. He employs the felicitous analogy of a poem in which nothing is said about the hero's having or lacking a sister. Here, obviously, the question whether the hero does have a sister has no answer, unless the author chooses to provide one.

The analogy is ingenious but it could be misleading. One notable difference is that the mathematician is answerable to empirical facts in a way that the poet is not. If mathematics is invented, it is with a view to its having a practical application. Wittgenstein himself is aware of this. 'Put two apples', he says, 'on a bare table, see that no one comes

---

[1] *Remarks*, p. 171.
[2] ibid., p. 47.

near them and nothing shakes the table, now put another two apples on the table; now count the apples that are there. You have made an experiment; the result of the counting is probably 4. (We should present the result like this: when in such-and-such circumstances, one puts first 2 apples and then another 2 on a table, mostly none disappear and none get added.) And analogous experiments can be carried out, with the same result, with all kinds of solid bodies. - This is how our children learn sums; for one makes them put down three beans and then another three beans and then count what is there. If the result at one time were 5, at another 7 (say because, *as we should now say*, one sometimes got added, and one sometimes vanished of itself), then the first thing we said would be that beans were no good for teaching sums. But if the same thing happened with sticks, fingers, lines and most other things, that would be the end of all sums.

' "But shouldn't we then still have $2 + 2 = 4$?" - This sentence would have become unusable.'[1]

The fact, acknowledged by Wittgenstein, that the utility of arithmetical sums depends upon certain physical circumstances, which might well have been otherwise, does not imply, nor does he take it to imply, that these sums are well-confirmed empirical generalizations, which is what they were believed to be by John Stuart Mill. The usual objection to this view is that it does not account for the necessity of mathematical propositions. Perhaps a better way of putting what prompts the objection is that it does not do justice to their normative character.

Mathematical propositions are normative inasmuch as they lay down rules for calculation. They are not predictions of what will result if anyone carried out certain operations, say that of addition or multiplication, for notoriously one can make mistakes in mathematics. Certainly, no one who maintains that mathematical propositions are necessarily true means to imply that a process of calculation, carried out by no matter whom, will inevitably yield a given result. The implication is rather that the rules which govern the calculation are such that only such and such an outcome is correct; anyone who comes up with a different answer is bound to have made a mistake.

Here Wittgenstein sees a problem. At the very outset of his remarks

[1] ibid., p. 14.

he raises the question how we use the expression 'The steps are determined by the formula'. *'How do I know'*, he asks, 'that in working out the series $+2$ I must write "20004, 20006", and not "20004, 20008"?'[1] He explains that he is not suggesting that when I come to '20004', I shall be in any doubt as to what the instruction to add 2 requires of me, that I shall hesitate between '20006' and '20008'. What he wants explained is the meaning of the statement that what is deemed the correct answer is predetermined by the imposition of the rule. 'My having no doubt', he says, 'in the face of the question does *not* mean that it has been answered in advance.'[2]

The problem is elusive, in the sense that it is not clear what would serve as its solution. We shall see that it reappears in the *Investigations*, and I shall have to say something more about it when I come to examine them. For the present I wish only to say that the difficulty seems to lie in reconciling the view that mathematics is a human invention with its seeming to compel us to accept certain conclusions, which in many cases we have to labour to discover. Thus, we are at liberty to define a prime number as one that is divisible only by 1 or itself, but having introduced this concept, we do not go on to control its application; we have to discover which numbers are prime. It might please us to think that there is a greatest prime number, and there would seem to be nothing in the concept of a prime number to prevent this. Unfortunately there is a proof, ascribed to Euclid, that there cannot be a greatest prime number. It runs very simply. Suppose that there were a greatest prime number. Let us call it n. Then let us multiply together all the numbers up to and including n and add 1. This number would be greater than n and since it will also be greater than the product of all its possible factors, it will itself be prime. Consequently n will not be the greatest prime number, however large a number it has been taken to represent.

If someone dislikes this conclusion, he may argue that it does not meet Wittgenstein's requirement that a proof be what Wittgenstein calls 'surveyable',[3] by which he appears to mean that it is the culmination of a traceable series of steps. Crispin Wright, who considers this argument, suggests that if n is made large enough, it may turn out

[1] *Remarks*, p. 3.
[2] ibid.
[3] ibid., p. 91.

to be beyond our powers to calculate the product of n and all its predecessors,[1] so that Euclid's proof could be dismissed as unsurveyable. Yet would not a classical mathematician regard this as irrelevant? He would claim to be able to see that Euclid's proof is valid. And I at least should hesitate to say that he was wrong.

We are brought to a similar impasse when we consider Wittgenstein's reaction to Gödel's theorem, which has been taken to show that in any system like Russell's and Whitehead's *Principia Mathematica*, which is rich enough to express arithmetic, one can construct a true proposition which is not provable within the system. In effect, this proposition, when translated out of its mathematical guise, asserts of itself that it is not so provable. This conclusion is unwelcome to Wittgenstein who wants to equate 'true in Russell's system' with 'proved in Russell's system'. Following his example, let us call Gödel's rogue proposition 'P'. Then Wittgenstein seems to alternate between allowing the mathematical authenticity of P but simply rejecting its interpretation into English as the statement that P is unprovable, and making light of the whole business. So far as I can follow his argument, he seems to me to favour the first of these courses, but the second is more in accordance with his general attitude. It is most clearly exhibited in the following paragraph:

Let us suppose I prove the improvability (in Russell's system) of P; then by this proof I have proved P. Now if this proof were one in Russell's system – I should in that case have proved at once that it belonged and did not belong to Russell's system. – That is what comes of making up such sentences. – But there is a contradiction here: – Well, then there is a contradiction here. Does it do any harm here?[2]

Wittgenstein takes this equally robust line with the semantic paradoxes. The following paragraphs, which succeed the one that I have just quoted, are typical.

Is there harm in the contradiction that arises when someone says 'I am lying – So I am not lying – So I am lying – etc' I mean: does it make our language less usable if in this case, according to the ordi-

[1] *Wittgenstein on the Foundations of Mathematics*, p. 138.
[2] *Remarks*, p. 51.

65

nary rules, a proposition yields its contradictory, and vice versa? – the proposition *itself* is unusable, and these inferences equally; but why should they not be made? – It is a profitless performance! – It is a language-game with some similarity to the game of thumb-catching.

Such a contradiction is of interest only because it has tormented people, and because this shows both how tormenting problems can grow out of language, and what kind of things can torment us.[1]

Mathematicians seek to prove the consistency of their systems, because they want them to be guaranteed against contradiction. And the reason why they attach so much importance to avoiding contradiction, is not just that a contradiction is bound to be false but that any proposition whatsoever is derivable from it. Consequently, it threatens the utility of the system as a whole. But do we have to take this threat so seriously? Why should we not put the contradiction, or the propositions from which it follows, as it were in quarantine? If we can separate them from the main body of the system, and we find that we can make a profitable use of what is left, why should we be debarred from doing so? It is not as if the possibility of constructing the paradox of the liar in English vitiated the whole language. If this is Wittgenstein's standpoint, I am in sympathy with it. But then I am not a mathematician.

[1] *Remarks*, pp. 51-2.

6

PHILOSOPHICAL INVESTIGATIONS

In 1945 when he seemed disposed to publish the first and major part, or something very like it, of what his executors released in 1953 as his *Philosophical Investigations*, Wittgenstein wrote a preface in which he described the work as the precipitate of investigations which had occupied him for the previous sixteen years. It is, therefore, not surprising to find an echo in the *Investigations* of the themes with which we have seen him to be occupied during that period. The technique is the same. Very often the same examples are used. We shall, however, find that certain lines of thought are more fully developed and their presentation made more emphatic. These are, principally, that the uses of language and of the signs which compose it are exceedingly diverse; that the results of philosophy, as correctly practised, consist in the exposure of the errors into which philosophers especially fall through misunderstanding the way their language works; that in philosophy we must do away with explanation and let description take its place, not seeking new information but arranging what we have always known; that we must avoid the mistake of trying to account for such things as understanding or intending by appealing to inner processes which explain nothing and need not occur at all; that the notion of following a rule is far more problematic than we might suppose; and that there cannot be a private language inasmuch as one cannot give oneself an ostensive definition. It is on these last points that I shall mainly be taking issue with him.

In many ways the *Investigations* is a repudiation of the *Tractatus* and becomes easier to understand when viewed in this light: so much so indeed that Wittgenstein is said to have favoured the idea of reprinting the *Tractatus* as a prelude to the *Investigations*, in their German texts. The breach is opened in the very first paragraph of the *Investiga-tions* which consists of a quotation from the *Confessions* of St Augus-tine and Wittgenstein's comments on the passage. He says that it paints a picture of language in which 'we find the roots of the following idea: Every word has a meaning. The meaning is correlated with the word. It is the object for which the word stands.'[1]

This is essentially the view of meaning that Wittgenstein took in the *Tractatus* and he now sets himself to show that it applies only to a fragment of language. For this purpose he resorts to his device of language-games, reviving the examples of *The Brown Book* and com-menting on them in the same fashion. Here he explicitly says that 'the term "language-*game*" is meant to bring into prominence the fact that the *speaking* of language is part of an activity, or of a form of life'[2] and he expatiates on the multiplicity of what he calls 'the tools in language and of the ways in which they are used'.[3]

In my description of the language-game in which proper names were introduced in *The Brown Book* I remarked that no provision was made for their use in the absence of the objects which they were intended to denote. This omission is made good in the *Investigations*. The example chosen is that of the sentence 'Moses did not exist', which Wittgenstein interprets as having various meanings. 'It may mean: the Israelites did not have a *single* leader when they withdrew from Egypt – or: their leader was not called Moses – or: there cannot have been anyone who accomplished all that the Bible relates of Moses – or: etc. etc.' [4] In short, he accepts Russell's view that a name like 'Moses' can be defined by means of various descriptions, so that a sentence containing the name acquires a different sense according to an adoption of one such description or another.

This may seem to raise a difficulty but Wittgenstein deals with it skilfully. 'But when', he affects to ask, 'I make a statement about Moses, – am I always ready to substitute some *one* of these descrip-tions for "Moses"? I shall perhaps say: By "Moses" I understand the man who did what the Bible relates of Moses, or at any rate a good deal of it. But how much? Have I decided how much must be proved

---

[1] *Philosophical Investigations*, I, para. 1.
[2] ibid., para. 23
[3] ibid.
[4] ibid., 79.

false for me to give up my proposition as false? Has the name Moses got a fixed and unequivocal use for me in all possible cases? – Is it not the case that I have, so to speak, a whole series of props in readiness, and am ready to lean on one if another should be taken from under me and vice versa?'[1]

In other words, a proper name does not lose or change its reference because some of the descriptions which are used to pick out its bearer miss the mark which the others hit. There is no standard measure for the degree of failure that is admissible before reference is lost. The decision is taken according to the circumstances of the case in question.

It follows, as Wittgenstein remarks, that a proper name 'is used without a *fixed* meaning'. It is characteristic of him to add, 'But that detracts as little from its usefulness, as it detracts from that of a table that it stands on four legs instead of three and so sometimes wobbles.'[2] We should note that he explicitly rejects the thesis that the meaning of a proper name is to be identified with its bearer and that he does not attempt to supply the bearers of names with essential properties, such as the circumstances of their origin, which are then supposed to determine the reference of the names. I am sure that he is right on both these counts.

Just as Wittgenstein has abandoned the search for the general form of propositions, which played so large a part in the *Tractatus*, and with it the idea of there being something common to everything we call language, rather than a multiplicity of relations, so he no longer insists on there being simple states of affairs to which the elementary propositions of the *Tractatus* were thought to correspond. Instead he argues, plausibly, that the distinction between what is simple and what is composite depends upon the way in which the question is raised, and indeed that the question has no meaning except within the rules of some language-game. 'But isn't a chessboard, for instance,' he asks, 'obviously, and absolutely, composite? – You are probably thinking of the composition out of thirty-two white and thirty-two black squares. But could we not also say, for instance, that it was composed of the colours black and white and the schema of squares? And if there are quite different ways of looking at it, do you still want to say that the

---

[1] ibid.
[2] ibid.

chessboard is absolutely "composite"?"[1] There may indeed be language-games to which the model of names corresponding to simple elements would be well suited. Wittgenstein devises an example where the sentence 'RRBGGGRWW' describes an arrangement of three rows of squares, coloured red, black, green, or white in the order which the sentence indicates. But while it would be natural in such a case to count the coloured squares as primary elements, it would still not be the only possibility.

Wittgenstein still feels the pull of the *Tractatus* to the extent that he is tempted to regard 'That is how things are' as the general form of a proposition and to equate this with defining a proposition as whatever can be true or false. It is noteworthy that he takes the 'reductionist' view of truth according to which '*p*' is true = *p* and '*p*' is false = not-*p*. This view works well so long as the proposition which is said to be true or false is explicitly mentioned, but is harder to accommodate to the cases where the proposition is not mentioned but only described as in the example 'Nothing that he told you is true'; for in these cases we have to make a further adjustment to the sentence in order to obtain an equivalent assertion when the predication of truth or false-hood has been struck out, and it is not obvious that this will always be feasible. Wittgenstein ignores this problem, but raises the objection that this way of attempting to capture the nature of a proposition is merely specious. It comes to no more, he says, than that 'we only predicate "true" and "false" of what we call a proposition. And', he continues, 'what a proposition is is in one sense determined by the rules of sentence formation (in English for example) and in another sense by the use of the sign in the language-game.' But then the trouble is that 'the use of the words "true" and "false" may [itself] be among the constituent parts of this game'.[2]

After a further review of the actual functioning of such concepts as those of reading and understanding, designed to show that they are not exhibited in simple mental acts, and culminating in the epigram 'In our failure to understand the use of a word we take it as the expression of a queer *process* (As we think of time as a queer medium, of the mind as a queer kind of being)',[3] Wittgenstein returns to one of

[1] *Investigations*, 47.
[2] ibid., 136.
[3] ibid., 196.

the main questions of his *Remarks on the Foundations of Mathematics:* what is comprised in obedience to a rule?

As this question occupies a central place in the *Investigations* I shall approach it by means of extensive quotations. At the end of paragraph 199 we find it asserted that 'To obey a rule, to make a report, to give an order, to play a game of chess, are *customs* (uses, institutions)', with the further comment: 'To understand a sentence means to understand a language. To understand a language means to be master of a technique.' There ensue descriptions of behaviour that might or might not be counted as conforming to the rules of chess, and then the following paragraphs:

> This was our paradox: no course of action could be determined by a rule, because every course of action can be made out to accord with the rule. The answer was: if everything can be made out to accord with the rule, then it can also be made out to conflict with it. And so there would be neither accord nor conflict here.
>
> It can be seen that there is a misunderstanding here from the mere fact that in the course of our argument we gave one interpretation after another; as if each one contented us at least for a moment, until we thought of yet another standing behind it. What this shews is that there is a way of grasping a rule which is *not* an *interpretation*, but which is exhibited in what we call 'obeying the rule' and 'going against it' in actual cases.
>
> Hence there is an inclination to say: every action according to the rule is an interpretation. But we ought to restrict the term 'interpretation' to the substitution of one expression of the rule for another.[1]
>
> And hence also 'obeying a rule' is a practice. And to *think* one is obeying a rule is not to obey a rule. Hence it is not possible to obey a rule 'privately': otherwise thinking one was obeying a rule would be the same thing as obeying it.[2]

It is these and similar passages in Wittgenstein's writings that have led Saul Kripke, in a stimulating book entitled *Wittgenstein on Rules and Private Language*, to propound the thesis that the nerve of Wittgenstein's argument against the possibility of private languages is to

[1] ibid., 201.
[2] ibid., 202.

be found in his treatment of the question of the observance of rules, and that his subsequent handling in the *Investigations* of the topic of the naming of sensations, on which discussions of Wittgenstein's 'private language argument' have most commonly been based, was intended only as a further illustration of a thesis which had already been proved. Whether or not Kripke is right on this historical point, which I am inclined to doubt, the considerations which he advances are worth examining for their own sakes.

Kripke's theory is that Wittgenstein is putting forward a radically sceptical argument, posing a problem to which he offers a sceptical solution. A sceptical solution is one that admits the cogency of the sceptic's argument but denies that this invalidates the beliefs which the sceptic has set out to demolish. The term 'sceptical solution' is taken from Hume's *Enquiries*, though there is no suggestion that Wittgenstein was consciously indebted to Hume, for whom there is evidence that he had no respect. All the same, Kripke thinks that Hume's interpretation of the necessary connexion which is supposed to obtain between cause and effect as consisting in nothing more than the habit of mind by which we associate types of events which we have found to be in constant conjunction, and his reliance on custom as the ground of our beliefs in default of any logical warrant that those conjunctions will continue to be constant, supply a precedent for Wittgenstein's treatment of the question of the correct observance of a rule.

The example which Kripke chooses to illustrate what he takes to be Wittgenstein's position is that of the sum '$57 + 68 = 125$'. This sum conforms to the rule of addition symbolized by ' $+$ ' but it also conforms to another rule symbolized by $\oplus$ according to which $x \oplus y = x + y$, provided that both $x + y$ are less than 57 but otherwise equals 5. Let us assume that our subject has never had occasion to calculate the sum of 57 and 68. It makes no difference to the argument whether the assumption is true or not; if it happens to be false there must, in view of the infinity of cardinal numbers, be some pair of numbers for which it holds good. Then the conclusion which Kripke attributes to Wittgenstein is that nothing in the subject's mental history or his past behaviour determines, in advance of his actually doing the sum, which rule he will follow; and this is taken to imply that so far as the subject's intentions were concerned there is, in a phrase given currency by Quine, no fact of the matter either.

As Kripke sees, this pattern of argument need not be confined to mathematics. It applies to semantics also. An example, which has made its way into philosophy, is that of the term 'grue' invented by Nelson Goodman,[1] thirty years ago, which applies to anything which is green and examined before a particular time t but otherwise to anything blue. So up to t the extensions of 'green' and 'grue' are indistinguishable. Suppose t to be the present. My inclination is to call grass green and the sky blue, but for all that I or anyone else can tell, this is not consistent with my past intentions. It may be that I always meant 'grue' by 'green' so that I should now be committed by my semantic rule to calling the grass blue and the sky green. Along those lines there is no settling the question one way or the other. Since a similar game can be played with any term one cares to choose we arrive at what Kripke takes to be the conclusion of Wittgenstein's sceptical argument that 'there can be no such thing as meaning anything by any word'.[2]

It is to be remarked that the scepticism which Kripke attributes to Wittgenstein goes much further than Hume's. Hume was not sceptical about causation: he noticed that no such thing as necessary connexion is observable in nature and so redefined the concept in such a way that it was capable of being satisfied. Hume was a sceptic about induction, inasmuch as he truly denied that there was any way of demonstrating or even showing it to be probable, without circularity, that the uniformities which we had hitherto detected would continue to obtain in future instances. On this point he anticipated Wittgenstein. But when Hume fell back upon custom he brought his scepticism to a halt. He did not query the right of any individual to say what his habits of association were, or what experiences had given rise to them. On the contrary, he ranked memory alongside perception as an immediate source of knowledge.

Hume's sceptical solution of his problem consists in the propensity attributed to each one of us to 'project' his past observations. In what is Wittgenstein's solution supposed to consist? The propositions which we endeavour to express are no longer accorded truth-conditions with which their meaning might be equated. How could they be if all facts of the matter have been done away with? What is put in their place is conditions of assertibility. And these are a matter of social agreement.

[1] See his *Fact, Fiction and Forecast*, ch. 3.
[2] Kripke, op. cit., p. 55.

The teacher judges that his pupil has mastered the rule of addition if he obtains enough of the same results as the teacher is himself disposed to reach. I am on the right semantic track so long as my verbal usages agree with those of my community.

This may sound very well, until we pause to consider what agreement comes to in this context. In the case of the teacher no provision has been made for anything more than the fact that on similar occasions he and his pupil make similar marks or noises. The practice of the community is supposed to bestow meaning on my utterances. But what is the community except a collection of persons? And if each of those persons is supposed to take his orders about meaning solely from the others, it follows that none of them takes any orders. The whole semantic house of cards is based upon our taking in each other's washing, or would be if there were any laundry to wash. On this interpretation, Wittgenstein's argument, so far from proving that private languages are impossible, proves that they are indispensable.

I turn now to what has usually been considered to be Wittgenstein's main argument against the possibility of a private language. There are, however, some points that need to be made clear first. To start with, Wittgenstein did not deny that we have sense-experiences, including sensations of pain and feelings of movement, or that these experiences are private in at least one reputable sense of the term. He may have imagined situations in which one would have a ground for saying that different persons shared their thoughts or sensations, but in the normal way he allowed each of us to have his own. Neither did he advance the view that a man's sensations and feelings, let alone his thoughts and images, are identical with physical events. He did not maintain that it is only if they are interpreted in physical terms, whether as referring to physiological states, or to dispositions to overt behaviour, that statements about one person's experiences can be made intelligible to another. There are passages in his works that might induce an unwary reader to take him for a physicalist, but in fact there is no evidence that he held even the milder thesis, which has recently come into fashion, that what are ordinarily classified as mental states are contingently identical with physical states of the brain.

The next point is more intricate. There are passages in the *Investigations* in which Wittgenstein appears to mean by a private language one that it is logically impossible for anyone but the speaker to understand.

If this were all that he meant, I doubt if anyone would dispute his claim that there can be no such language. Certainly I should not wish to do so. Neither do I seek to deny that, as a matter of fact, one's references to one's private experiences are made within the framework of a public language. What I am querying is Wittgenstein's assumption that this is a logical necessity. The view which I am attributing to him is that it would not be possible to frame concepts only on the basis of one's own experience; if the signs in which such concepts were supposed to be embodied constituted a 'private language' in this sense, they would not have any meaning even for their author himself.

The argument in favour of this position is most forcibly set out in paragraph 258 of the *Investigations*. 'Let us', says Wittgenstein, 'imagine the following case. I want to keep a diary about the recurrence of a certain sensation. To this end I associate it with the sign "E" and write this sign in a calendar for every day on which I have the sensation. – I will remark first of all that a definition of the sign cannot be formulated. – But still I can give myself a kind of ostensive definition. – How? Can I point to the sensation? Not in the ordinary sense. But I speak, or write the sign down, and at the same time I concentrate my attention on the sensation – and so, as it were, point to it inwardly. – But what is this ceremony for? for that is all it seems to be! A definition surely serves to establish the meaning of a sign. Well, that is done precisely by the concentration of my attention; for in this way I impress on myself the connexion between the sign and the sensation. – But "I impress it on myself" can only mean: this process brings it about that I remember the connexion *right* in the future. But in the present case I have no criterion of correctness. One would like to say: whatever is going to seem right to me is right. And that only means that here we can't talk about "right".'

But why could one not rely on one's own memory to furnish a criterion of correctness? It need not be confined to linking a single present with a single past sensation. To a very large extent sensations of similar types occur in groups. So one memory could be checked by another. Wittgenstein considers this suggestion and rejects it. He produces the example of a man's attempting to check his memory of the time of a train departure by calling to mind an image of the time-table and dismisses it with the comment that 'this process has got to produce a memory which is actually *correct*. If the mental image of the time-table could not itself be *tested* for correctness, how could it confirm the correctness of the first memory? (As if someone were to buy several copies of the morning paper to assure himself that what it said was true.) Looking up a table in the imagination is no more looking up a table than the image of the result of an imagined experiment is the result of an experiment.'[1]

The simile of the morning paper is brilliant but I am still not convinced by the argument which it is meant to serve. The crucial fact which it seems to me that Wittgenstein persistently overlooks is that anyone's significant use of language must depend sooner or later on his performing what I call an act of primary recognition. In Wittgenstein's example, it is supposed not to be sufficient for someone to check his memory of the time at which the train is due to leave by visualizing a page of the time-table. He has to check the memory in its turn by actually looking up the page. This would, indeed, be a sensible measure to take. But unless he can trust his eyesight at this point, unless he can recognize the figures printed in the table, he will be no better off. If he distrusts his eyesight, as well as his memory, he can consult other people, but then he must understand their responses; he needs to identify correctly the signs that they make. The point I am stressing is not the trivial one that the series of checks cannot continue indefinitely in practice, even if there is no limit to them in theory, but rather that unless it is brought to a close at some stage the whole series counts for nothing. Everything hangs in the air unless there is at least one item that is straightforwardly identified.

If this is correct, Wittgenstein is wrong in taking the corroboration of one memory by another, or that of a memory by an item of sense-experience, as an inferior substitute for some other method of verification. There is no other method. Whatever I have to identify, whether it be an object, an event, an image, or a sign, I have only my memory and my current sensation to rely on. There is a difference only in the degree to which the memories and sensations are cross-checked.

I think it very important to note that it makes no difference to my present argument whether it is applied to the use of signs to refer to what are counted as public objects or to their use to refer to so-called private experiences. If my apparent reference to a public object is

---

[1] *Investigations*, para. 265.

judged by those who share my language to be deviant, they can explain this in various ways. They may ascribe to me a false belief, arising perhaps from some defect in perception, or they may judge that I am lying to them, or else that I am making a linguistic error. Which explanation they adopt will depend upon the circumstances of the case. In the same way, if they take me to be honest, they have to decide whether it is my use of words or my sensations themselves that are deviant when I report them in ways that do not consort with their observations of my behaviour. Again their decision will depend upon the circumstances of the case.

This does concede the point, on which Wittgenstein repeatedly insists, that we should not in practice be able to learn and teach the word for sensations like pain unless they were outwardly manifested. Indeed, Wittgenstein's preference for pain as an example is no doubt due to the fact that it is characteristically associated with a fairly limited set of outward expressions; something which is not true of all sensations, let alone thoughts and images. Nevertheless, just as we are taught the use of words that refer to physical objects by being placed in situations where we undergo sense-experiences which are held to correspond with those of our teachers, so we are supplied with a vocabulary for describing our mental life through analogies which are drawn from our behaviour. In particular, we learn the use of the words which stand for various types of thought in relation to the acts of speaking and writing which are counted as their expressions, to the circumstances in which these expressions occur, and to the behaviour with which they are causally connected. Wittgenstein's well-known dictum, 'An "inner process" stands in need of outward criteria', is pedagogically true.

What is not true, in my opinion, is the assumption, which Wittgenstein often appears to make, that the meaning of words is indissolubly tied to the contexts in which they are originally learned. An obvious counter-example is our understanding of references to the past. No doubt a child's conception of the past is originally linked to the exercise of his memory. It is by having his attention drawn to events which his teacher expects him to remember that he learns the use of the past tense. This does not prevent him from being able quite soon to distinguish between past events in general and the very small fraction of them which he remembers; and once he has succeeded in making this distinction he can come to understand that even when he does remember an event, his remembering it is not a necessary condition of its being past. In the same way, it can be conceded that a causal condition of my coming to understand the use of the English word 'pain' consisted in the fact that when I felt pain, as a child, I behaved in ways that my elders took to be the expression of it. This does not, however, in the least prevent me from drawing a present distinction between my feelings of pain and the behaviour which expresses them, so that when I ascribe pain to myself I refer to the feeling and not to its manifest effects. For reasons on which I have already touched, I believe that I am able to make the same distinction when I attribute pain to others. I should, indeed, be puzzled if someone regularly claimed to be in great pain and yet exhibited none of the signs which it is ordinarily thought to produce. I should also be puzzled if he exhibited the signs while denying that he felt any pain. If I did not suspect his honesty, I should probably conclude that he had not mastered the use of the word 'pain'. All the same, the hypothesis that the ordinary link between pain and its manifestations is missing in his case does not seem to me to be excluded: I do not find it unintelligible.

Once again, this puts me at odds with Wittgenstein. We have seen that he wrestled in *The Blue Book* with the problem attending our ascription of experiences to others and he returns to it in the *Investigations* as an offshoot of his campaign against the possibility of private languages. His argument is most forcibly developed in the following much-quoted paragraph:

If I say of myself that it is only from my own case that I know what the word 'pain' means – must I not say the same of other people too? And how can I generalize the *one* case so irresponsibly?

Now someone tells me that *he* knows what pain is only from his own case! – Suppose everyone had a box with something in it: we call it a 'beetle'. No one can look into anyone else's box, and everyone says he knows what a beetle is only by looking at *his* beetle. – Here it would be quite possible for everyone to have something different in his box. One might even imagine such a thing constantly changing. – But suppose the word 'beetle' had a use in these people's language? – If so it would not be used as the name of a thing. The thing in the box has no place in the language-game at all; not even as a *something*: for the box might even be empty. –

No, one can 'divide through' by the thing in the box; it cancels out, whatever it is.

That is to say: if we construe the grammar of the expression of sensation on the model of 'object and name' the object drops out of consideration as irrelevant.[1]

This looks like a commitment to behaviourism, but the ensuing paragraphs do not wholly bear it out. They appear rather to hover over it. Wittgenstein admits that there is a very great difference between pain-behaviour accompanied by pain and pain-behaviour without any pain, but when he goes on to speak of the sensation, as distinct from the behaviour, the best he can do is to say that 'It is not a *something*, but not a *nothing* either.'[2] Again, in the case of remembering, he insists that he is not denying the occurrence of an inner process. 'What we deny is that the picture of the inner process gives us the correct idea of the use of the word "to remember".'[3] As in *The Blue Book*, he finds difficulty in the notion of one's imagining another person's pain. 'If', he says, 'one has to imagine someone else's pain on the model of one's own, this is none too easy a thing to do: for I have to imagine pain which I *do not feel* on the model of the pain which I *do feel*. That is, what I have to do is not simply to make a transition in imagination from one place of pain to another. As, from pain in the hand to pain in the arm. For I am not to imagine that I feel pain in some region of his body (which would also be possible). Pain-behaviour can point to a painful place – but the subject of pain is the person who gives it expression.'[4]

This seems to lead to a position which we have seen to be untenable; the adoption of a behaviouristic account of the experiences of others and a mentalistic account of one's own. There are passages in the *Investigations* which make me suspect that Wittgenstein has fallen into this trap, but again the evidence is inconclusive. As we saw a moment ago, a case can also be made for labelling him a consistent behaviourist. Indeed, he goes so far as to have this question put to him, only to give a teasing answer. '"Are you not really a behaviourist in disguise? Aren't you at bottom really saying that everything except human be-

[1] *Investigations*, 293.
[2] ibid., 304.
[3] ibid., 305.
[4] ibid., 302.

haviour is a fiction?" If I do speak of a fiction, then it is of a *grammatical* fiction.'[1]

So now the secret is out. We look to have the grammar made clear to us. But that is just what Wittgenstein fails to do. There follows a paragraph in which it is obscurely suggested that the root of the trouble lies in some naive misunderstanding of our talk about states and processes, and then the most celebrated of his gnomic utterances: 'What is your aim in philosophy? To show the fly the way out of the fly-bottle.'[2]

For my own part, I am not at all affronted by the comparison of myself, when I am at grips with a philosophical problem, to an insect that is seemingly entrapped. If I have any grievance against Wittgenstein in this regard, it is that, in my case at least, he fails to achieve his aim; he does not reveal to me the avenue of escape. One reason for this is that I decline to take what he repeatedly indicates as the all-important first step, the rejection of the idea of the private ostensive definition. As I hinted earlier on when I tried to rebut Wittgenstein's general argument against the possibility of a private language, I think that he is misled by his use of the word 'private'. An object like a tea-cup is said to be public because there is sufficient agreement in the reports of different observers on a series of occasions to give us a motive for saying that they perceive the same tea-cup. In the case of a headache this motive is lacking, and therefore we say that headaches are private. Nevertheless, in both cases, the meaning which any one of us attaches to the word is 'cashed', to echo William James, in terms of his own experience.

This last point is repeatedly contested throughout the *Investigations*, either directly or by implication. A good example occurs in paragraph 377: 'What is the criterion for the sameness of two images? – What is the criterion for the redness of an image? For me, when it is someone else's image: what he says and does. For myself, when it is my image: nothing. And what goes for "red" also goes for "same".'

If Wittgenstein wishes to equate my criterion for the acceptance of the statement that some other person is experiencing a red image with the meaning that I attach to the statement, the argument which I have

---

[1] *Investigations*, 307.
[2] ibid., 309.

developed against a behaviouristic interpretation of the references that one makes to the experiences of other persons would show him to be wrong. Neither is it clear how I manage to interpret the sayings and doings of another person as his possession of a red image, possibly one of the same colour as I am myself experiencing, if I have no criteria, in my own case, for the application of either 'red' or 'same'. Wittgenstein deals with this objection in his own fashion by having someone ask 'How do I know that this colour is red?' and replying 'It would be an answer to say "I have learnt English".'[1] How good an answer would this be if the man were blind?

In the *Investigations*, as in *The Blue Book*, Wittgenstein links what he regards as the solipsistic tendencies of those who insist on the privacy of experience with peculiarities in the use of the first person pronoun. This comes out in various places, notably the following paragraph:

When I say 'I am in pain', I do not point to a person who is in pain, since in a certain sense I have no idea *who* is. And this can be given a justification. For the main point is: I did not say that such-and-such a person was in pain, but 'I am ...'. Now in saying this I don't name any person. Just as I don't name anyone when I *groan* with pain. Though someone else sees who is in pain from the groaning.

What does it mean to know *who* is in pain? It means, for example, to know which man in this room is in pain: for instance, that it is the one who is sitting over there, or the one who is standing in that corner, the tall one over there with the fair hair, and so on. – What am I getting at? At the fact that there is a great variety of criteria for personal '*identity*'.

Now which of them determines my saying that 'I' am in pain? None.[2]

Now it is quite correct to assert that when I say 'I am in pain' I do not name any person, if all that is meant is that the English word 'I', like other demonstratives, does not fall into the class of proper names. On the other hand, it seems strange to deny that I point to any person, and to take as the ground for this denial my having no idea, in a

[1] ibid., 381.
[2] ibid., 404.

certain sense, *who* is in pain. What is the force here of the qualification 'in a certain sense'? I do not suppose that it relates to the cases where I have lost my memory, or undergone some deception, so that I am mistaken about or ignorant of my own identity. For in the first place these cases are uncommon, whereas Wittgenstein seems to be claiming that, in the sense he has in mind, the person who says 'I am in pain' never has an idea who it is, and anyhow even in the uncommon cases there seems no question but that the author of the sentence does point to a person to whom he ascribes pain. I suspect that what Wittgenstein had in mind was that the word 'I', in this usage, is not linked to any description, so that the truth of the proposition expressed by the sentence 'I am in pain' is independent of the question who I am. If I am right in this conjecture, Wittgenstein would have done better to say that the author of the sentence need have no idea who is in pain rather than that in a certain sense he has none. Moreover, it will still be a mistake to deny that the word 'I' in such a sentence serves to point to a person to whom pain is ascribed.

It is sometimes asserted that the word 'I', in English, differs from other demonstratives in that its use, when not an avowed pretence as in a work of fiction, cannot suffer a failure of reference. I think that this is false on two counts. On the one hand I believe that, if fiction is excluded, the demonstrative 'now' is bound to succeed in its reference, for any utterance must be made at some time or other and the word 'now', and its equivalents in other languages, are understood to refer to the times of the utterances at which they occur. On the other hand, I do not believe that the word 'I' and its equivalents are guaranteed the same success. Examples of this failure would be those cases in which the word is sincerely used by a medium to refer not to herself but to a spirit which she and perhaps others also believe to be making use of her voice as an instrument, whereas no such spirit exists. The same examples would destroy the immunity as a demonstrative of the word 'here' and its equivalents, since the spirit might be credited with using the word to refer to its place in a non-existent world. Such examples approximate to fiction, except that they are not intended to be fictional. They bear some resemblance also to quoted usages where a remark in the first person can easily be attributed to someone who did not make it or even to someone who does not exist at all.

If 'I' has an advantage over other personal pronouns it is that I cannot be in error in using it to indicate myself, at least so long as I do not characterize myself further than as the person whom I am now using the word 'I' to indicate. It cannot be true that I am really indicating another person or failing to indicate anyone. In the case of the second person pronoun I can use it in error to address some object, or deity, or phantom that does not exist. In the case of the third I run the risk of referring to the 'wrong' object as well as that of referring to what does not exist. So there is this difference, but the qualifications needed to bestow security on the use of the first person singular seem to me to deprive it of any consequence. Not only is my existence, whatever that amounts to, presupposed in the statement of the claim but we also refuse to bind either 'I' or 'myself' to any informative description. For once we allow such descriptions in, the avenues to error are all laid open.

In any case, whatever needs to be said about our use of pronouns, it seems to have no essential bearing on the question of solipsism. Even if we always used proper names to refer to ourselves and one another, as children sometimes do, we should still have our several experiences, and this is all that the problems arising from the apparent opposition of our capacity for knowing our own experiences to our capacity for knowing the experiences of others require to get them posed. Since one of Wittgenstein's principal objects in his later writings is to dissolve this set of problems, we shall return to them again.

Towards the end of the first part of the *Investigations* Wittgenstein adverts to the subject of willing. Unfortunately he is here at his most cryptic, and though he devotes several pages to the topic, it is not at all clear, to me at any rate, what moral we are meant to draw from them. Among the remarks he makes are that it makes no sense to speak of willing willing and that this is connected with the fact that it is a mistake 'to think of willing as an immediate non causal bringing about',[1] that my raising my arm is not the result of my willing that it shall go up [2] and that 'voluntary movement is marked by the absence of surprise'.[3] On the whole it looks as if this is another skirmish in his campaign against the failure of philosophers to do justice to the diversity of the phenomena which our language invites them to assemble

---

[1] *Investigations*, 613
[2] ibid., 616.
[3] ibid., 628.

under the heading of a species of mental act. He makes the same point at considerable length, in the cases of expecting, believing, intending, remembering and various emotional attitudes. One of the morals which he wishes his readers to draw is expressed succinctly in paragraph 655: 'The question is not one of explaining a language-game by means of our experiences, but of noting a language-game.' It is a recurrent tactic of Wittgenstein's to pretend that he limits himself to description of various practices and does not proceed to criticize them or theorize about them. Yet by now it should be obvious that his work is permeated with theory, and with criticism too, mostly indeed of the theories built upon our linguistic practices, but in a way also of the practices themselves in so far as they foster what he regards as misdescription. What makes his own theories difficult to pin down is that they are repeatedly insinuated by mainly felicitous examples, very seldom expounded or defended by a train of continuous argument.

A good illustration of Wittgenstein's misuse of his all-purpose concept of a language-game occurs near the beginning of the second part of the *Investigations* in his treatment of the subject of dreams. I quote the relevant passage in full:

People who on waking tell us certain incidents (that they have been in such and such places, etc.). Then we teach them the expression 'I dreamt', which precedes the narrative. Afterwards I sometimes ask them 'did you dream anything last night?' and am answered yes or no, sometimes with an account of a dream, sometimes not. That is the language-game. (I have assumed here that I do not dream myself. But then, nor do I ever have the feeling of an invisible presence; other people do, and I can question them about their experiences.)

Now must I make some assumption about whether people are deceived by their memories or not; whether they really had these images while they slept, or whether it merely seems so to them on waking? And what meaning has this question? – And what interest? Do we ever ask ourselves this when someone is telling us his dream? And if not – is it because we are sure his memory won't have deceived him? (And suppose it were a man with a quite specially bad memory? –)

Does this mean that it is nonsense ever to raise the question whether dreams really take place during sleep, or are a memory phenomenon of the awakened? It will turn on the use of the question.[1]

The truth which prompts these reflections is that children learn to employ and understand the vocabulary of dreaming by reporting experiences which they seem to remember undergoing while they were asleep, and by being taught by their elders to distinguish these experiences both from their waking fantasies and principally from the experiences which they have been taught to regard as their past perceptions of actual events. Almost all the suggestions that Wittgenstein develops from this basis are false. From the fact that the concept of dreaming is acquired in this fashion it does not in the least follow that when the possessors of it refer to their own or other persons' dreams they are making any allusion whatsoever to any tendency to report them. As it happens, this tendency is not at all widespread. What most frequently happens is that one wakes with a consciousness of having dreamt, but almost immediately forgets the content of the dream. Exceptions to this rule are persons who are subservient to their psycho-analysts and, more rarely nowadays, those who believe that dreams foretell the future. Persons of both these sorts and those who attach the corresponding importance to their narratives have a strong interest in their being truthful. The narrators of dreams may well have motives for lying about them; but the lie will consist in falsifying the memory of a dream, not in representing as a dream what was actually a wakeful memory. But does it make sense to say that one might be honestly mistaken in one's memory of a dream? No less sense than it makes to say that one misremembers one's past thoughts or feelings. Indeed the possibility in the case of the dream is the more open to verification, inasmuch as the dreamer's subsequent report may conflict with what he has been overheard to say in his sleep or what is later elicited from him by hypnosis. What I find hard to envisage is the mistaking of a delusive waking memory for the memory of a dream, but I suppose that a highly suggestible subject could be put into this position by a fervent psycho-analyst. Where I quarrel with Wittgenstein is in his suggesting that this is a standing dilemma. I fail also to see the point of his pretending that he is not himself a dreamer, unless the implication is that it would make no difference to his mastery of

[1] *Philosophical Investigations*, II, section VII.

the concept of dreaming, in which case I should again take issue with him. The analogy of having the feeling of an invisible presence does not seem to me adequate. I have once undergone this illusion, when I was visiting Mycenae, and I am sure that this has given me a measure of understanding that I should not otherwise have had.

For the most part the remarks that have been put together to form the second part of the *Investigations* reiterate points on which we have already touched. The most notable exception is the set of comments focusing upon the celebrated example of the duck-rabbit, a drawing which is seen by different observers, or by the same observer at different times, as depicting either the head of a rabbit or that of a duck. The problem is to describe what it is for the drawing, or other puzzle pictures of a familiar character, to appear as this or that, and in particular to give an illuminating account of the shift in their aspects.

It might indeed seem that examples of this sort brought grist to the mill of the sense-datum theorist. He would find no difficulty in supposing that one and the same drawing could evoke different sense-experiences on different occasions. This is not, however, an approach that Wittgenstein could tolerate. 'And above all,' he warns us, 'do *not* say "After all my visual impression isn't the drawing: it is *this* – which I can't show to anyone". Of course it is not the drawing, but neither is it anything of the same category which I carry within myself.'[1] His strongest argument in support of the prohibition is that if one were required to sketch these respective sense-impressions all that would emerge in each case would be something like the original problem-picture. To which it appears to me that the sense-datum theorist could reply that the difference in the sense-impressions consists in a difference of focus which could indeed be described but need not be reproducible in a drawing. But perhaps Wittgenstein himself has a better answer. What he says is that 'The expression of a change of aspect is the expression of a *new* perception and at the same time of the perception's being unchanged.'[2] In view of the overall failure of Wittgenstein's campaign against private languages, I think that the advantage rests with the sense-datum theorist.

[1] *Investigations*, section XI, p. 196.
[2] ibid.

7

ON MAGIC AND RELIGION

We have seen that when Wittgenstein lectured on ethics soon after his return to Cambridge, he did not develop any kind of moral theory, but drew the attention of his audience to types of experience which he chose to describe in religious terms. We have also seen that he did not try to make the occurrence of such experiences the basis of any argument in favour of religious belief. His declaration that those who tried to talk about ethics and religion tended to run against the boundaries of language implied that no such arguments could possibly be valid. It is obvious that no argument can establish the truth of a nonsensical conclusion. What we found puzzling was that this did not lead Wittgenstein, as it did such logical positivists as Neurath and myself, simply to dismiss religious doctrines, along with the rest of metaphysics, as not worth serious attention, except perhaps for sociologists. Wittgenstein's conception of important nonsense remains mysterious.

I doubt if there is any way of vindicating this conception, but some light may be thrown upon it by examining Wittgenstein's reactions to his reading of the single-volume abridged edition of Sir James Frazer's *The Golden Bough*. Wittgenstein's series of remarks on this topic are included in a hodge-podge of essays about his life and work compiled by C.G. Luckhardt and published in 1977 under the overall title of *Wittgenstein: Sources and Perspectives*.

It is well known that Frazer starts with the story of the King of the Wood at Nemi whose slaying by his successor, who is destined to be slain in his turn, is treated by Frazer as a rite of spring: the succession of the kings is designed to secure the succession of the crops. Frazer dealt in the same way with many other practices of ritual. He treated them as exercises of magic and looked upon magic as simple-minded science. One might wonder why the primitive men, who furnished Frazer with his material, did not lose their faith in magic when they discovered that it did not work, but the answer is that it did work, or at least that it was not found to fail. As Frazer put it, 'A ceremony intended to make the wind blow or the rain fall, or to work the death of an enemy, will always be followed, sooner or later, by the occurrence it is meant to bring to pass; and primitive man may be excused for regarding the occurrence as the direct result of the ceremony, and the best possible proof of its efficacy.'[1]

Wittgenstein takes strong exception to this whole approach. His reason for finding Frazer's account of 'the magical and religious views of mankind' unsatisfactory is that it makes them look like errors. 'Was Augustine in error, then,' he asks, 'when he called upon God on every page of the Confessions?'[2] We are expected to find it obvious that Augustine was not in error, but not to infer from this that he was speaking the truth. Otherwise we should come up against the difficulty that men of other religious faiths, say Buddhists quite as sincere and intelligent as Augustine, have advanced very different views. What right have we to say that they were in error? Wittgenstein's answer is that we again have none. Neither Augustine nor the Buddhist was in error, 'except when he set forth a theory'.[3] The implication is that one need not be committing oneself to any theory when one engages in religious practices or when one expresses religious beliefs. Even when the members of different sects appear to contradict one another, neither party need be in error. That it is equally the case that neither party need be asserting any truth is a point that Wittgenstein fails to stress.

What applies to religion, according to Wittgenstein, applies equally to magic:

The very idea of wanting to explain a practice – for example, the killing of the priest king – seems wrong to me. All that Frazer does is to make them plausible to people who think as he does. It is very remarkable that in the final analysis all these practices are presented as, so to speak, pieces of stupidity. But it will never be plausible to say that mankind does all that out of sheer stupidity.

[1] *The Golden Bough*, p. 59.
[2] *Wittgenstein: Sources and Perspectives*, p. 61.
[3] ibid.

When, for example, he explains to us that the king must be killed in his prime, because the savages believe that otherwise his soul would not be kept fresh, all one can say is: where that practice and these views occur together, the practice does not spring from the view, but they are both just there.

It can indeed happen, and often does to-day, that a person will give up a practice after he has recognized an error on which it was based. But this happens only where calling someone's attention to his error is enough to turn him from his way of behaving. But this is not the case with the religious practices of a people and *therefore* there is *no* question of an error.

Frazer says it is hard to discover the error in magic – and that is why it has lasted so long – because, for example, an incantation that is supposed to bring rain certainly seems efficacious sooner or later. But then it is surely remarkable that people don't realize earlier that sooner or later it's going to rain anyhow.[1]

I do not find this so remarkable. If the believers in the efficacy of the rain dance never omit to perform it, what ground do they have for concluding that the rain would arrive anyway? One might despise them for failing to experiment, omitting the ceremony for once and seeing what happened, but this could well be a risk that they were not prepared to take. If their survival depended on the rain, and they firmly believed that but for their performance of the rain dance the rain would not come, would it be rational for them to make the experiment? Is it always rational to test one's beliefs? The cost of the test has to be considered. Unless I wished to commit suicide, and did not command an easier way to die, it would not be rational for me to jump out of the window in order to test the law of gravitation.

Wittgenstein refers later on to the example 'of a Rain-King in Africa to whom the people pray for rain when the *rainy period comes*', arguing:

But surely that means that they do not really believe that he can make it rain, otherwise they would make it rain in the dry periods of the year in which the land is 'a parched and evil desert'. For if one assumes that the people formerly instituted this office of Rain-King out of stupidity, it is nevertheless clear that they had pre-

[1] ibid., pp. 61–2.

viously experienced that the rains began in March, and then they would have had the Rain-King function for the other part of the year.[1]

Again, I do not find this argument conclusive. We are not bound to suppose that these people began with the observation that the rain fell only at certain seasons, and then limited their propitiation of the Rain-King to the times when they already had inductive grounds for believing that the rain would fall. Neither need we credit them with the belief that they controlled the Rain-King by their ceremonies. They may have been animists from the start and discovered inductively that it was only at certain seasons that the Rain-King was in the mood to be propitiated, or possessed the power to perform his office. Once again, the crucial experiment would be their omitting to perform the ceremony at the appropriate time and finding that it made no difference, and again they might reasonably have been afraid to run the risk.

I question also whether one is entitled to assert, so categorically as we have seen that Wittgenstein does, that people are not deterred from religious practices by the breakdown of a theory which they previously held. The behaviour of Anglicans in the last hundred and fifty years tells a more complicated story. It is true that many of them, especially in recent times, are willing to allow that the account of creation, as given in the Book of Genesis, should not be taken literally. The story of Adam and Eve is said to be a myth: so also, by some bolder spirits, is the story of the Virgin Birth. Nevertheless there have been many and still are some for whom the biblical account of creation does operate as a theory. The development of palaeontology and the theory of evolution are seen as threatening their faith: in many cases acceptance of these scientific theories has destroyed it. Similarly while there may not be many Anglicans nowadays who feel obliged to take a literal view of the Virgin Birth, I suspect that it is only a minority who would be content to treat the story of the Resurrection so cavalierly. If it could be shown to them to be a fiction, they would lose their faith. And once they had lost their faith, I doubt if very many of them would continue their religious practices.

Wittgenstein argues against Frazer that the skills displayed by pri-

[1] *Wittgenstein: Sources and Perspectives*, p. 72.

mitive people are inconsistent with an unscientific belief in the efficacy of magic. 'The same savage', he says, 'who stabs the picture of his enemy apparently in order to kill him, really builds his hut out of wood and carves his arrow skilfully and not in effigy.' The suggestion is that the stabbing of the picture is a mere venting of the agent's spleen, a symbolic act, not seriously expected to have any practical effect. It would appear, however, that this is not the general view of such actions in the communities where they are practised. The savage who learns that an enemy to whom he attributes magical powers has fashioned and stabbed his image has been known to sicken and die. Neither do we need to penetrate the jungle of anthropology in order to expose the weakness of Wittgenstein's argument. Technology in Europe was quite well developed by the seventeenth century, yet this did not prevent the existence of a widespread belief in the potency of witchcraft. Those accused of being witches were not tortured and burned for their performance of symbolic acts; they were thought to work actual mischief. Again, astrology is not scientifically respectable: yet it has commanded very wide credence down to the present day. The natives of southern India possess advanced technological and artistic skills yet there are many things that they will not do, such as celebrating marriages, unless the situation of the stars is thought to be propitious. Nor is this just a symbolic observance. It is believed that if the stars are flouted actual misfortunes will follow.

This is not to say that ritual is never purely symbolic. A good example of Frazer's, which Wittgenstein cites,[1] is that of a practice formerly prevalent in Bulgaria and among the Bosnian Turks. 'A woman will take a boy whom she intends to adopt and push or pull him through her clothes; ever afterwards he is regarded as her very son, and inherits the whole property of his adoptive parents.' Here it would indeed be absurd to credit the women with the belief that she was actually giving birth to the child, but here too the symbolism is easy to interpret. The woman's imitation of the process of birth solemnizes her intention to treat the boy as if he actually were her son.

Wittgenstein speaks very harshly of Frazer, accusing him of leading 'a narrow spiritual life' and saying that Frazer 'cannot imagine a priest who is not basically a present-day English parson with the same stu-

---

[1] ibid., p. 65.

pidity and dullness':[1] yet he does little to explain the symbolism which he blames Frazer for failing to discuss. 'Why shouldn't it be possible', he asks, 'for a person to regard his name as sacred? It is certainly, on the one hand, the most important instrument which is given to him, and, on the other, like a piece of jewelry hung around his neck at birth.'[2] But treating a God's name as sacred, in the case of the Jews at least, involved keeping it hidden, and this is seldom true of one's own name, unless one is ashamed of it, in which case one may get it changed. And why should it be considered the most important instrument that one receives? It is indeed important for the part it plays in making one the object of linguistic reference, but does this count for more than one's appearance or genetic inheritance? I do not know how such a question should be argued and Wittgenstein does not argue it.

Some writers on religion have sought to take advantage of Wittgenstein's concept of a language-game. They have argued that religious beliefs are not to be assessed from the outside. They are embedded in a language-game which is essentially characterized by the deliverance of certain answers to the questions posed in the course of playing it and their accompaniment by various forms of ritual, and that is all there is to it. This position has the advantage of being thoroughly ecumenical. There need be no more discussion between Protestants and Roman Catholics, or between Hindus and Muslims, than there is between those who like playing poker and those who like playing chess. All the same I am surprised that religious believers find it satisfactory. I am not myself a religious believer but if I were I doubt if I should be content to be told that I was playing a game in accordance with a canonical set of rules. Rather, I should wish for some assurance that my beliefs were true.

[1] *Wittgenstein: Sources and Perspectives*, p. 65
[2] ibid.

8

THE PHILOSOPHY OF PSYCHOLOGY

Towards the middle of the *Tractatus*, after stating that philosophy is not a theory but an activity and that the object of philosophy is the logical clarification of thoughts, Wittgenstein proceeds to give his view of the relation of philosophy to psychology. It consists of three remarks, combined in the single paragraph numbered 4.1121; they run as follows:

> Psychology is no more closely related to philosophy than is any other natural science.
>
> Theory of knowledge is the philosophy of psychology.
>
> Does not my study of sign-language correspond to the study of thought-processes, which philosophers used to consider so essential to the philosophy of logic? Only in most cases they got entangled in unessential psychological investigations, and with my method too there is an analogous risk.

In view of the first two of these remarks, it is interesting to note first that with the exception of his incursions into the foundations of mathematics, almost all of Wittgenstein's work, after he returned to Cambridge in 1929, was concerned with the philosophy of psychology, and secondly that so far from identifying the philosophy of psychology with what had commonly passed for the theory of knowledge, he was increasingly disposed to treat questions about the status of our claims to knowledge as either uninteresting or improper. What appears in its place is an investigation into our use of psychological concepts. This is not a psychological investigation, in the sense that it takes much account of the researches of practising psychologists, though some attention is paid to the theories and experiments of *gestalt* psychologists. There are a good many imaginary experiments, but they are woven into what Wittgenstein in the *Tractatus* called his study of sign-language: in his later idiom they might be said to feature in various language-games.

Wittgenstein was most fully occupied with the philosophy of psychology, in the foregoing sense, during the period 1946–8. Some of the notes which he then compiled foreshadowed the second part of the *Investigations*. The duck-rabbit, for example, already makes its appearance. Some made their way into *Zettel*, the collection of fragments which two of his literary executors, Anscombe and von Wright, assembled and published, as we have already noted, in 1967. The same two executors later decided to publish both the typescripts, from which the remarks had been extracted, in full. They appeared in 1980 in two volumes under the overall title of *Remarks on the Philosophy of Psychology*. The precedent set in the *Tractatus* of having the German text and the English translation on facing pages was again observed. The first volume was edited by Anscombe and von Wright and translated by Anscombe. It consists of 1137 remarks, occupying 198 double pages. The second volume, which is shorter, consisting of 737 remarks on 121 double pages, was edited by von Wright and Heikki Nyman and translated by C.G. Luckhardt and M.A.E. Aue. Neither volume is easy reading. Not that many of the remarks are obscure in themselves. The trouble is that, even less than in the *Investigations*, does their sequence pursue a linear course, and that while many of the tales are adorned very few of the morals are pointed. In justice to Wittgenstein, it should be remembered that it was not his but his executors' decision to publish these musings in the form in which he left them.

At one point in the first volume the translator faced a difficulty. No distinction is commonly made in translation between the German words *Erlebnis* and *Erfahrung*. They are both rendered by the English word 'experience'. In this passage, however, Wittgenstein contrasts them and lays weight upon the contrast. Anscombe responds by keeping 'experience' as the English equivalent of *Erlebnis*, and using 'undergoing' to translate *Erfahrung*. In its English version the remark accordingly runs as follows:

Ought I to call the whole field of the psychological that of 'experience'? And so all psychological verbs 'verbs of experience'. ('Concepts of experience') Their characteristic is this, that their third person but not their first person is stated on grounds of observation. That observation is observation of behaviour. A subclass of concepts of experience is formed by the 'concepts of undergoing'. 'Undergoings' have duration and a course: they may run on uniformly or non-uniformly. They have intensity. They are not characters of thought. Images are undergoings. A subclass of 'undergoings' are 'impressions'. Impressions have spatial and temporal relations to one another. There are blend-impressions. E.G. blends of smells, colours, sounds. 'Emotions' are 'experiences' but not 'undergoings'. (Examples: sadness, joy, grief, delight.) And one might distinguish between 'directed emotions' and 'undirected emotions'. An emotion has duration; it has no place; it has characteristic 'undergoings' and thoughts; it has a characteristic expression which one would use in *miming* it. Talking under particular circumstances, and whatever else corresponds to that, is thinking. Emotions colour thoughts. One sub-class of 'experiences' is the forms of conviction. (Belief, certainty, doubt etc.) Their expression is an expression of thoughts. They are not 'colourings' of thoughts. The directed emotions might also be called 'attitudes'. Surprise and fright are attitudes too, and so are admiration and enjoyment.[1]

Somewhat similar claims are made in a plan for the treatment of psychological concepts which is set out in two long and more than usually discursive paragraphs of the second volume of remarks.[2] In this case psychological verbs are said to be characterized by the fact that the third person of the present tense is to be identified by sensation, the first person not. Otherwise the main contentions are that sensations have duration and degree; that one knows the position of one's limbs and their movements; that pain is differentiated from other sensations by having a characteristic expression; that sensations give us knowledge about the external world, whereas emotions and images do not; that images are subject to the will; that they are not distinguished from sensations by their vivacity nor is their reference secured by their resemblance to what is imagined; that besides having characteristic

[1] *Remarks on the Foundations of Psychology*, I, para. 836.
[2] ibid., II, para. 63 and 148.

expressions emotions issue in characteristic behaviour; and that when they are directed upon objects, these objects may but need not be their causes.

There is nothing in all this to which I see any reason to take exception, though much that calls for further exploration. For instance, we need to learn more about the nature and function of images, the various processes of thought, and the way in which sensations give us knowledge of the external world. It is noteworthy that both series of pronouncements begin with a reference to the distinction between the use of verbs in the first and the third person. I take it that the same point is being made in both cases, though the difference in the two formulations leaves some room for doubt. In the passage cited from the first volume, it is not explicitly asserted, as it is in the other, that we are concerned only with the present tense but I think that this can safely be assumed. The mention in the first passage of different persons being 'stated' on different grounds sounds strange in English but the use of the German word 'ausgesprochen', which 'stated' is meant to translate, suggests to me that the reference is to the different ways in which the identity of the subject of the verb is thought to be decided, rather than to an alleged difference in the grounds on which the statements in the different persons are made. It does not greatly matter whether I am wrong in my interpretation, as the second point is also one that we shall need to consider.

The suggestion, then, which I now propose to examine is that the distinctive characteristic of 'psychological verbs', equated with 'verbs of experience', is that when they are used in the third person of the present tense the subject to whom the experience is being attributed is identified by observation, and specifically by observation of the subject's behaviour, whereas this is not true when the attribution is made in the first person of the present tense to the person himself.

As it stands, this suggestion is plainly false. Whether I am attributing an experience to him or not, the subject to whom I am referring by the use of a verb in the third person present can be identified in all manner of ways, other than by his current behaviour. If it is only my own identification of him that is in question I can in many cases identify him simply by his appearance. If it is a matter of identifying him at large, I can use a demonstrative, perhaps accompanied by a gesture, I can take hold of him, in some contexts I can point to a label that he is wearing. I should normally have at my disposal a variety of descriptions which he is known or can be seen to satisfy. As for statements made in the first person, they do not have to ascribe experiences, or indeed be made by sentences in the present tense, for their author to be able to construe them, without recourse to observation, as referring to himself. As far as others are concerned, however, his use of the first person identifies him only demonstratively, and it is also quite consistent with an inability to identify himself, in the sense that owing, perhaps, to a loss of memory, he does not know who he is.

This attempted characterization of psychological verbs is so patently inadequate that we must look for another interpretation of Wittgenstein's remarks. I conjecture that what he may have had in mind, even though it is not what he actually wrote, is that the identification of a subject *as* the owner of whatever experience the use of a sentence in the present tense is ascribing to him is effected by observation when the sentence is in the third person but not when it is in the first. In short, the distinction is supposed to turn not on the difference in the way the owner of an experience, ascribed to him by a sentence in the first or third person of the present tense, is identified by himself or others, but on a difference in which the ascriptions made in these different ways are respectively verified. The contrast is not indeed just between the use of the first and third persons in the present tense, but between the use of the first person and any other. It is maintained that to ascertain the truth or falsehood of a statement in which I ascribe a present experience to some other person I have to rely on observation, whereas this is not the case when I am making the ascription to myself.

How clear is this dictinction and how far is it acceptable? There is indeed a peculiarity in our use of the first person in the present tense. If I make an assertion in this manner the content of which is that I am entertaining such and such thoughts, have acquired such and such beliefs, have formed such and such intentions, am undergoing such and such sense-experiences, including kinaesthetic sensations, or am having the sensations which go together with my feeling such and such emotions, then my assertion is grounded on its content. I should like to say that if such assertions are honestly made, there is no possibility of their being false, were it not that I can misdescribe my sense-experiences and my sensations, and I am not entirely convinced that this is in all cases simply a matter of an idiosyncratic use of words. Un-happily, I also think that I can be mistaken about my intentions, if only in exceptional cases, and also about my beliefs. I do not think that my claims to believe whatever it may be are always immune from self-deception. I am debarred therefore from maintaining that the pe-culiarity of psychological statements honestly made in the first person by sentences in the present tense is that their author possesses a guar-antee of their truth. What I should prefer to say is that, so far as their author is concerned, they are distinguished by the immediacy of their content. In the old-fashioned terminology of Russell and Moore, the speaker is acquainted with their content in a way in which he cannot be acquainted with the thoughts, beliefs, intentions, sensations or sense-experiences of another person.

I am far from satisfied with this formulation and wish that I could improve upon it. At best it may serve me as a stimulus towards clari-fying some of the issues which I take to be in question.

In the first place I am well aware that in allowing a person to have what Ryle called privileged access to his own thoughts and sensations I am taking up a position which Wittgenstein believed himself to have refuted. I have, however, already given my reasons for not succumbing to his private-language argument. He trades on this argument at vari-ous points in the course of this collection of remarks. I think that it will be enough to quote one of the sharpest of them: 'Always eliminate the private object for yourself, by supposing that it keeps on altering: you don't notice this, however, because your memory keeps on deceiv-ing you.'[1]

This is characteristically ingenious, but once more my response is that it proves too much. I can equally well suppose that a public object, like the glass from which I am drinking, the table at which I am writing, the watch on my wrist, continually changes in a way that would put it beyond recognition if my memory were not correspond-ingly deceptive. Again it will be said that in the case of the public object it is the agreement of other observers who also claim to see the object in question that puts the hypothesis that my memory is con-stantly deceiving me out of court, or anyhow deprives it of any interest. If our reports of our observations are in agreement, then it does not

[1] *Remarks*, I, 985.

matter what their respective contents are; indeed, it might be argued that the identification of the contents themselves, the 'sense-impressions' of red or cold or hard or whatever, itself depends on agreement in predicating them of public objects.[1] And once again I protest that the fact of agreement has itself to be established, and that there is no other way of establishing it except through sense-experience. Wittgenstein's argument is again frustrated by the need for what I have called an act of primary recognition.

If we do allow there to be a sense in which one does have privileged access to one's own thoughts and sensations, are we to regard this as an empirical or a conceptual truth? And if it is a conceptual truth, does it depend on our electing to play a particular language-game, one that requires us to discriminate between the use of the first and second or third persons in the present tenses of a particular class of verbs? This does not sound right; so narrowly linguistic an account seems not to get to the root of the distinction; surely it would still obtain if we lacked demonstratives and verbal inflexions and relied instead on proper names or even only on descriptions and spatio-temporal co-ordinates to pinpoint our references. This would, indeed, not prevent the distribution of experiential contents among different persons from being conceptual. At the same time, in this as in other cases, the conceptual necessity would be sustained by the empirical facts. If we were not self-conscious and if our thoughts and bodily sensations tallied to the same extent as the sense-experiences on which our perceptions of physical objects are founded, then we should have no occasion for devising a language which made provision for the separation of different streams of consciousness. But would it not still be possible to distinguish the way in which an object appeared to one person from the way in which it appeared to another? It would still be possible but the motive for drawing such distinctions would be lacking.

But is it only my own states of consciousness with which I can plausibly be said to be directly acquainted? At least at one point Wittgenstein appears to suggest that this is not so:

Consciousness in the face of another. Look into someone else's face and see the consciousness in it, and also a particular *shade* of con-

[1] cf. I, 896.

sciousness. You see on it, in it, joy, indifference, interest, excitement, dullness, etc. The light in the face of another.

Do you look within *yourself*, in order to recognize the fury in *his* face? It is there as clearly as in your own breast.

(And what does one want to say? That someone else's face stimulates me to imitate it, and so that I feel small movements and muscular tensions on my own part, and *mean* the sum of these? Nonsense! Nonsense, – for you are making suppositions instead of just describing. If your head is haunted by explanations here, you will neglect to bear in mind the facts which are most important.)[1]

Certainly, I do not want to say that I detect fear or anger or joy in the face of another person on the basis of my own kinaesthetic sensations. I do not want to say even that I am engaged in making any conscious inference, any more than I am when I identify the physical objects which surround me. Nevertheless, I am prepared to say that I make an unconscious inference, in the sense that I take it for granted that my reading of the other person's expression will be corroborated by his behaviour, just as I take it for granted that my interpretation of the visual impressions on the basis of which I identify the physical objects will be corroborated by further sense-impressions of the appropriate kind. The analogy breaks down if I also regard myself as making an unconscious inference to the existence of feelings in the other person which go with the emotion that I read in his face. I believe that I am taking such a step when I attribute the emotion to him. For example, it is the main factor that distinguishes my 'seeing' an emotion in the face of another living person and my 'seeing' the same emotion in the face of a character in a strip cartoon.

If sensations are said to give us knowledge of the external world, it is not how Wittgenstein meant them to be distinguished from observations. I hesitate to saddle him with my own view that observations incorporate sense-impressions but go beyond them in 'positing' external objects, but it seems to me that he would have been impelled towards some view of this sort, if he had fully carried out his plan for the treatment of psychological concepts. As it is, we need raise no objection to its being said that we observe the external objects that we perceive predominantly by sight, but do not observe, or do not nor-

[1] I, 927.

mally observe, our seeing them. I put in the qualification because of the possibility of playing games with mirrors. It might be objected that the most I can achieve with mirrors is to observe myself looking at an object, not actually seeing it, but this is not a line that I think Wittgenstein would have cared to take, inasmuch as it puts the perceptions of others beyond the reach of my observation. It would lead me to say that I observed another person's looking at an object but not his seeing it. Touch also presents a problem since I surely can observe my hand in contact with an object which I am touching. It may be argued that it is only the sensation that counts, but again this is going to create a difficulty when it comes to my observation of other persons. Surely Wittgenstein would have wanted to say that I observed their touching physical objects, not merely their being in physical contact with them. Perhaps the best to be made of his position is to say that by his reckoning 'see' and 'touch' are not psychological verbs; what is psychological is to have visual or tactual sense-impressions. It will be for his followers to avoid letting this draw them into the admission of privileged access.

If the exclusion of verbs like 'see' and 'touch' might be thought to make Wittgenstein's characterization of psychological verbs too restrictive, there are also grounds for thinking it too generous. I take it that observation is contrasted with kinaesthetic sensation and while a statement like 'I have a headache' might pass for being psychological, statements like 'I am frowning' or 'I am sneezing' would not, though they too are expressed in the first person present and accepted on the basis of kinaesthetic sensation. Of course these are not statements that anyone would ordinarily make, but that is beside the point. As we have already implied, the question at issue is not simply one of a difference in the use of sentences of different forms but rather one of a difference in the grounds for accepting different beliefs.

Wittgenstein appears to have attached considerable importance to what he called 'Moore's paradox'; the oddity of affirming a proposition and going on to say that one does not believe it. There is, indeed, no denying that such statements as 'It will rain this afternoon but I do not believe that it will' do sound strange. They are not self-contradictory. It may well be the case both that it will rain this afternoon and that I do not believe that it will. In short, both parties to the conjunction may be true; the appearance of contradiction, or at least of paradox, arises only from the fact of my conjoining them. Again, for those who like to view things linguistically, this is a peculiarity of the use of the present tense of the verb 'believe' in the first person. There is nothing odd about saying 'It will rain this afternoon, though the meteorologists do not believe that it will' or 'It rained yesterday, though I did not believe that it would'. It would, however, be misleading to represent this as an oddity of grammar. What Moore's so-called paradox brings to light is a social convention. The convention does not operate in all contexts. It may be obvious that I am speaking ironically, or I may be enacting a part on the stage, or giving an illustration in a lecture, or repeating a quotation; but in the normal way, when I utter a sentence in the form of an assertion, it is assumed that I believe what I say. More often than not, it is my intention to express the belief, but this need not be so. A liar takes advantage of the convention. It is important not to confuse the observance of the convention with a point of logic. My act of making the assertion is a conventional sign that I believe what I am saying, but the assertion itself, for example, that it will rain this afternoon, does not logically entail that I believe it. This is proved by the fact that my going on to assert that I do not believe what I have just asserted does not issue in a contradiction.

In all this there is no serious paradox. There is simply the fact that one's belief in one's own assertion is neither explicitly stated nor logically assumed, but conventionally implied. Curiously enough, as I shall remark again,[1] an actual assertion of belief is conventionally taken as implying a lesser degree of confidence in what follows. It is understood as suggesting some degree of doubt.

It might be suggested that Moore's paradox could take a stronger form. Though there is a greater likelihood that both parties to the conjunction will be true, since more is required for knowledge than for belief, there is still an oddity about saying such things as 'It will rain tomorrow but I do not know that it will'. One would expect such a guarded assertion to be made in the form 'It will probably rain tomorrow' or even 'I believe that it will rain tomorrow but of course I don't know that it will'. Again, this is not merely a matter of linguistic usage. When the assertion is such that its author is thought to

[1] cf. p. 110.

be qualified to know its truth, as in the case of a common-sense statement like 'The ink-pot is on the table' or a well-authenticated historical claim like 'The Battle of Waterloo was fought in 1815', there is a conventional implication that the speaker knows the truth of what he is asserting, and also that he intends to convey the knowledge. This does not apply to cases like that of the prediction of rain, where the most that is accorded to him is the right to hold and convey a belief. For some reason, ordinary linguistic usage is accommodated to the first and not the second of these two sorts of instances.

Wittgenstein goes astray here. After listing the three sentences 'It's going to rain' – 'Do you believe it's going to rain?' – 'I know it's going to rain', he alleges that the third sentence is a repetition of the first and a rejection of the second.[1] He is wrong on both counts. The third sentence is not just a repetition of the first, but goes beyond it. Neither does the third sentence reject the second, in the sense of entailing a negative answer to the question. All that it does is to remove the suggestion of doubt which the affirmation of belief is apt to carry.

In the following paragraph Wittgenstein appears to go even further astray by adopting the Platonic view of knowledge as an infallible state of mind. A reference to what is almost a repetition of the passage in *Zettel*[2] suggests, however, that he is setting out the view for criticism rather than espousing it. Even so, his verdict is not entirely hostile. His conclusion is not, as I shall argue later[3] that the Platonic view is mistaken but that it 'does indeed point to one kind of use for "I know". "I know that it is so" then means: it is so, or else I'm crazy.' 'So', he continues, 'when I say, without lying: "I know that it is so," then only through a special sort of blindness can I be wrong.' I suppose that the special sort of blindness goes along with the special sense of 'I know' if such there be. As the word is ordinarily used, I can go wrong in a more humdrum fashion by not having the right sort of evidence, or more often by suffering the misfortune of claiming to know what is not in fact the case.

A number of Wittgenstein's remarks on the philosophy of psychology are remarks about thinking, some of which are reproduced more succinctly in *Zettel*. Their upshot, which occurs in the same form

[1] II, para. 302.
[2] para. 408.
[3] See p. 115.

in both works, is this: 'Thinking, a widely ramified concept. A concept that comprises many manifestations of life. The phenomena of thinking are widely scattered.'[1] When it comes to the question whether thinking is an experience, there is a remark covering two paragraphs in the psychology notes, of which the first is set out in *Zettel*.[2] I find the longer version more instructive:

> But why do I want to say that thinking is not an experience? – One can think of 'duration'. If I had spoken a whole sentence instead of the single word, I couldn't call one particular point of time in which I was thinking the beginning of my thinking process, nor yet the moment in which it took place. Or, if one calls the beginning and end of the sentence the beginning and end of the thought, then it is not clear whether one should say of the experience of thinking that it is uniform during this time, or whether it is a process like speaking the sentence itself.
>
> Sure, if we are to speak of an *experience* of thinking, the experience of speaking is as good as any. But the concept 'thinking' is not a concept of experience. For we don't compare thoughts in the same way as we compare experiences.[3]

There had been a time, while he was excogitating the *Tractatus*, when Wittgenstein had conceived of thinking as a kind of speaking, aloud or to oneself. Thirty years later he had become convinced that the concepts of thinking and speaking are '*categorially* different'.[4] This must not, however, lead us to suppose either that thinking is an accompaniment of speaking or that it is a process that can proceed unaccompanied. In the end we are brought back to something very like the view that Wittgenstein claims to have discarded. 'The word "thinking"', we are told, 'can be used to signify, roughly speaking, a talking for a purpose, i.e. a speaking or writing, a speaking in the imagination, a "speaking in the head", as it were.'[5] I should call this a lame and impotent conclusion, if I had anything better to put in its place.

[1] *Remarks*, II, para. 220. *Zettel*, para. 110.
[2] *Zettel*, para. 96.
[3] *Remarks*, II, 257.
[4] ibid., II, 7.
[5] ibid., II, 9.

In view of what he wrote in the *Investigations* about dreaming,[1] a passage which has misled at least one of his disciples into identifying the content of a dream with a report, made on waking, of something that never occurred, it is a relief to discover that both in his psychological remarks[2] and in very nearly the same words in *Zettel*,[3] Wittgenstein rejects this identification:

Let us imagine a tribe of men, unacquainted with dreams, who hear our narration of dreams. One of us had come to these non-dreaming people and learnt bit by bit to make himself understood to them – Perhaps one thinks they would never understand the word 'to dream'. But they would soon find a use for it. And their doctors might well be interested in the phenomenon and might make important inferences from the dreams of the stranger – Nor can it be said that for these people the verb 'to dream' could mean nothing but: to tell a dream. For the stranger would of course use both expressions, both 'to dream' and 'to tell a dream', and the people of that tribe would not be allowed to confuse 'I dreamt ...' with 'I told the dream ...'.[4]

If this confusion could be avoided by those who did not dream, how much more easily can it be avoided by those who do.

We have seen that Wittgenstein has some fruitful ideas about images, but it can hardly be claimed that his treatment of them covers all the ground. They are, indeed, subject to the will in a way in which sense-impressions, including kinaesthetic sensations, are not. These cannot be conjured up, in the way that images can. Nevertheless it is not true that they are always subject to the will. Day-dreams afford an exception and so do the unpleasant images that sometimes force themselves upon us. Neither do most of us control the images that we see on the cinema or on television screens. We can, indeed, abstain from viewing them, but equally we can put ourselves out of the way of receiving the sense-impressions which afford us access to the external world. Neither need there be any intrinsic difference between them. An image may masquerade as a sense-impression. It is true that for the

[1] Part II, section VII. And see above, pp. 84-5.
[2] *Remarks*, I, 101.
[3] para. 530.
[4] *Zettel*, para. 530.

most part, an impression of one of the 'external' senses promotes a belief in the presence of a physical object, whereas the entertaining of an image does not, but this is not invariably so. For instance, a visual impression of a scene viewed through a telescope and an image of the same scene viewed on television need differ only in their causal provenance. In the case of memory images it is not so much a matter of their causes as their effects. They prompt belief in the occurrence of past events which they are interpreted as portraying. A point which Wittgenstein rightly stresses is that it is not in virtue of any intrinsic feature that they refer to the past.

It may come as a surprise to contemporary philosophers that Wittgenstein, so far from subscribing to the fashionable theory of psychophysical identity, is sceptical about the likelihood of there being psycho-physical laws. Indeed, he puts it more strongly:

> Thinking in terms of physiological processes is extremely dangerous in connexion with the clarification of conceptual problems in psychology. Thinking in physiological hypotheses deludes us sometimes with false difficulties, sometimes with false solutions. The best prophylactic against this is the thought that I don't know at all whether the humans I am acquainted with actually have a nervous system.[1]

This is, indeed, a startling thought but the possibility of entertaining it proves no more than that there is no logical connexion between mental processes and whatever physical processes might be thought to be their counterparts. It does not prove that they are not empirically connected. Even this, however, is a hypothesis that Wittgenstein is prepared to question. In a paragraph which is reproduced word for word in *Zettel*, he asserts:

> No supposition seems to me more natural than that there is no process in the brain correlated with associating or with thinking; so that it would be impossible to read off thought-processes from brain-processes. I mean this: if I talk or write there is, I assume, a system of impulses going out from my brain and correlated with my

[1] *Remarks*, I, 1063.

spoken or written thoughts. But why should the *system* continue further in the direction of the centre?[1]

This seems to allow for what is currently known as token-token identity, a random identification of thoughts and other mental states with contemporary states of the brain. What it puts in question is the existence of a systematic correlation, a necessary basis for the theory known as that of type-type identity, which alone is of scientific interest. We should note that Wittgenstein does not deny the truth of systematic psycho/physical parallelism, which is a matter for scientific investigation. He merely seeks to remove the *a priori* prejudice which many people have in its favour.

More surprisingly he adopts a similar attitude to the question of memory. The relevant passage is again reproduced in *Zettel*. It runs as follows:

> I saw this man years ago: now I have seen him again, I recognize him, I remember his name. And why does there have to be a cause of this remembering in my nervous system? Why must something or other, whatever it may be, be stored-up there *in any form*? Why *must* a trace have been left behind? Why should there not be a psychological regularity to which *no* physiological regularity corresponds? If this upsets our concept of causality then it is high time it was upset.[2]

Once more, the question of there being a physiological explanation is one for scientific enquiry. Wittgenstein is concerned only to uproot the *a priori* assumption that there has to be one. It is not very often that I agree with him, but here I sympathize with his iconoclasm.

[1] ibid., I, 903, also *Zettel*, para. 608.
[2] ibid., I, 905, also *Zettel*, para. 610.

9

KNOWLEDGE AND CERTAINTY

I have tried to show that the arguments which Wittgenstein directs against the possibility of a private language are not convincing. A related question, which I have not yet fully explored, is that of one's knowledge of one's own experiences. This is often thought to be connected with their privacy. Wittgenstein in the *Investigations* takes note of the assumption that one has what Ryle called privileged access to one's own sensations and deals with it in summary fashion:

> In what sense are my sensations *private?* – Well, only I can know whether I am really in pain; another person can only surmise it. – In one way this is false, and in another nonsense. If we are using the word 'to know' as it is normally used (and how else are we to use it?), then other people very often know when I am in pain. – Yes, but all the same not with the certainty with which I know it myself! – It can't be said of me at all (except perhaps as a joke) that I *know* I am in pain. What is it supposed to mean – except perhaps that I *am* in pain?
>
> Other people cannot be said to learn of my sensations *only* from my behaviour, – for *I* cannot be said to learn of them. I *have* them.
>
> The truth is: it makes sense to say about other people that they doubt whether I am in pain: but not to say it about myself.[1]

This contrasts with what we have seen to be Wittgenstein's more elaborate treatment in *The Blue Book* of the problem of one's knowledge of the experiences of others, and it seems to me a change for the worse. To begin with, even if it were true that I cannot be said to have knowledge of my own sensations, which I shall in fact argue not to be

[1] *Philosophical Investigations*, I, para. 246.

the case, nothing would follow about the grounds for ascribing knowledge of them to persons other than myself. In particular, it would not
follow that they learned of them otherwise than by observation of my
behaviour. This is not to deny them the possibility of other sources of
such information. I am not maintaining that they could not have
physiological or even telepathic evidence. I am concerned only to expose the inadequacy of Wittgenstein's argument.

It may be that Wittgenstein is right in claiming that while it makes
sense to say that I doubt whether some other person is in pain, it
would be senseless for me to say this about myself, though this is not
a view that commands universal agreement. For example, pragmatists
like C.S. Peirce and C.I. Lewis have asserted that all judgements,
including judgements about one's own current sensations, are fallible.
There is indeed no question but that one can be in doubt as to the
correct description of an experience, say a sensation of colour, that
one is currently undergoing, but one might set such cases aside as
irrelevant to the present issue, on the ground that doubts of this sort
relate only to one's choice of words, not to any matter of fact. I am
not fully persuaded that this is so but am content to leave the question
in abeyance, since whichever way it is decided, the answer will not
support Wittgenstein's contention that 'it can't be said of me at all
(except perhaps as a joke) that I *know* I am in pain'.

But would not Wittgenstein be right if it made no sense to say of
someone that he was in pain but did not know it? No, he would not.
The most that would follow would be that being in pain entailed
knowing that this was so. In fact, I do not believe that this entailment
holds. The point is disputable, but I am inclined to hold that sentient
creatures, whether human or animal, without the command of language, can truly be said to be in pain without knowing it. What can
be conceded is that if someone is credited with the mastery of a natural
language and also with speaking honestly, then his saying in that
language that he knows that he is in pain supplies no further information than his simply saying that he is in pain. But so far from its
following that his saying that he knows himself to be in pain is senseless, it follows that it is true. Whether his statement is or is not
intended as a joke is totally irrelevant.

What has led Wittgenstein astray here, and not here alone, is that
there is seldom any point, outside the practice of philosophy, in for-

mulating such a sentence as 'I know that I am in pain'. One might assert it in protest against an unduly hearty nurse, or in attempting to undermine the confidence of an experimental psychologist, or in argument with a Christian Scientist, but the range of occasions for its appropriate use is admittedly narrow. It does not in the least follow that it cannot be used, with perfect semantic propriety, to state what is true.

We can go still further. Even if there were never any point, apart from the provision of a philosophical example, in asserting a claim to some item of knowledge, it would not follow that the claim was invalid. This can be illustrated by another instance. Although people most commonly believe what they assert, the conventional effect of prefacing a sentence with the words 'I believe that' is to weaken the force of the assertion which it is used to make. Its addition suggests that one is not entirely sure of what follows. For example, if I were to say 'I believe that Paris is smaller than London', I should commit myself less than by saying outright 'Paris is smaller than London'. Nevertheless, it surely does not follow that when I do assert something outright, I do not believe it. A similar feature of our use of the verb 'to believe' is that it is commonly taken as showing an unwillingness to make a claim to knowledge. Because our conventional practice is not to make a weaker claim when we think that we are in a position to make a stronger one, to say 'I believe' suggests that I lack the confidence to say 'I know'. All the same, I could not properly be said to know that such and such was the case, if I did not even believe it to be so. It should by now be apparent that its being pointless or even misleading for me to say such things as 'I know that I have a headache' or 'I know that this spot looks red to me' in no way entails that what I am saying is not true.

In the notes collected by his executors to form the volume *On Certainty*, which we have remarked that Wittgenstein is believed to have composed during the last eighteen months of his life, he extends the range of the restrictions that he seeks to impose upon our talk of knowledge. He bases his arguments upon G.E. Moore's celebrated defence of common sense.[1] Notoriously, Moore had attempted to safeguard what he called the common-sense view of the world against the

[1] See G.E. Moore, 'A Defence of Common Sense', *Philosophical Papers*, pp. 32–59.

arguments of philosophers who doubted or denied it simply by claiming that he knew it to be true.

In the course of lectures entitled *Some Main Problems of Philosophy* which he delivered in the winter of 1910-11, though they were not published as a book until 1953, Moore made it clear that he equated the common-sense view of the world with the acceptance of three very general beliefs. The first of these beliefs was, in his own words, 'that there are in the universe enormous numbers of material objects'.[1] He did not attempt to define what he meant by a material object, but he gave as examples, human bodies, animals, plants, mountains, grains of sand, minerals, drops of water, manufactured articles, such as machines and pieces of furniture, together with the sun, the stars and the earth. All these things were held to be located in a single space and time.

The second belief was that men, and perhaps some other animals, have minds, which Moore took as meaning that they perform what he called acts of consciousness. Again, he offered no definition of what he understood by acts of consciousness, but gave as examples, hearing, seeing, remembering, feeling, thinking and dreaming. Somewhat surprisingly, he took it to be a common-sense belief that such acts of consciousness are located not only in time but in space, their spatial positions being identified with those of the bodies of the creatures that perform them. Moore also ascribed to common sense the belief that acts of consciousness are attached to bodies in the sense of being causally dependent upon them, but that the bodies of which this is true form only a small proportion of material objects. The common-sense opinion was justly taken to be that whereas material objects of many different sorts are among the things upon which acts of consciousness are directed, in the vast majority of cases they are not equipped to perform any such acts, and they can also exist without there being any consciousness of them.

The third of the general beliefs in which Moore took the common-sense view of the world to consist was the belief that we really do know that there are material bodies and that there are acts of consciousness and in both cases that they have the properties which he has attributed to them. To this should be added the belief that 'we

[1] *Some Main Problems of Philosophy*, p. 12.

know an immense number of details about particular material objects and acts of consciousness, past, present and future'.[1] It was, indeed, from the truth of the more specific propositions in which our knowledge of such details is embodied that Moore professed to deduce the truth of the more general propositions which served for him to exemplify the standpoint of common sense.

His method is set out most clearly in his essay 'A Defence of Common Sense', which originally appeared in 1925 in the second series of *Contemporary British Philosophy*, before being reproduced in the posthumous collection of his *Philosophical Papers*. It consists in giving a long list of propositions, of the truth of every one of which he claimed to have certain knowledge. The propositions are divided into two classes. The facts which were taken to be expressed by the members of the first class were, to start with, that there existed and had existed for some time a body which was Moore's body; that throughout the time of its existence this body had been in contact with or not far from the surface of the earth; that there had existed many other things, also having shape and size in three dimensions, from which Moore's body had been at various distances and with some of which it had been in contact; that among these things there had been many other human bodies of which similar propositions were true; that many of these bodies had ceased to exist; that the earth had existed for many years before Moore was born; and that during many of those years a large number of human bodies had at every moment been alive upon it, and had, in very many cases, ceased to exist before Moore was born.

A continuation of the first class of propositions was that since his birth Moore had had many different experiences; that he had often perceived his own body, and other things in his environment, including other human bodies; that he had often observed facts about those things, such as the fact, which he was observing as he wrote, that a particular mantelpiece was nearer to his body than a particular bookcase; that he was aware of facts which he was not currently observing, such as that his body had existed on the previous day and had then been for some time nearer to the mantelpiece than to the bookcase; that he had had expectations with regard to the future; that he had held many beliefs, both true and false; that he had thought of imagi-

[1] *Some Main Problems of Philosophy*, p. 12.

nary things without believing in their reality; that he had had dreams, that he had had feelings of many kinds; and that many other human beings had had similar experiences.

The second class had only one member. That was the proposition which stated it to be true of many human beings, who satisfied propositions corresponding, in their cases, to the propositions of the first class which Moore had asserted of himself, that each of them had frequently known such propositions to be true.

Moore thought that his common-sense view of the world needed defence against two groups of metaphysicians: those who denied the existence of space and time and matter, and those who held that while propositions implying the existence of space and time and matter might be true, none of us knew them to be so. He accused the second group of self-contradiction on the rather dubious ground that their use of the first person plural implied that they knew that they and other persons existed, and that the existence of persons entailed the existence of material objects situated in space and time. This charge could not be brought against the first group who did not make any show of referring to themselves, but Moore impaled them also on what he took to be the fact that persons were material objects, since it followed from this that if their theory was true no philosopher could have existed to hold it. In fact the metaphysicians whom Moore was attacking would not have acquiesced in the concept of a person on which his arguments depended. If they were followers of Descartes they would regard themselves as spiritual substances, committed thereby to the existence of time but not to that of space or matter. If they were Absolute Idealists they would be dispensing with the categories of space, time and matter altogether. What Moore's arguments came down to was a simple denial of their right to do so.

The same underlying simplicity is manifested in Moore's 'Proof of an External World', a lecture delivered to the British Academy in 1939, and also reproduced in his *Philosophical Papers*. 'I can', he told his audience, 'prove now, for instance, that two human hands exist. How? By holding up my two hands, and saying, as I make a certain gesture with the right hand, "Here is one hand", and adding, as I make a certain gesture with the left, "And here is another". And, if by doing this, I have proved *ipso facto* the existence of external things, you will see that I can also do it now in numbers of other ways: there is no need to multiply examples.'[1] And a little later Moore went on to prove that material objects had existed in the past by reminding his audience that he had held up his hands a few minutes earlier.

The point of this whole procedure is that if Moore really did know what he claimed to know, it would follow that any philosopher who denied the truth of Moore's common-sense propositions, or even expressed doubt as to their truth, must be mistaken. For what is known to be true cannot fail to be so, whatever may be urged against it. So it would appear that the question to be answered is whether Moore was justified in making his claims to knowledge.

In his notes *On Certainty*, Wittgenstein does address himself to this question, but only in a roundabout fashion. His main object is to show that it does not seriously arise. He does not deny that the propositions on Moore's list were true or even that their truth could be held to be certain. On the contrary, he maintains that in normal circumstances to express any doubt of their truth would be nonsensical. Where he parts company with Moore is in holding that if it were significant to express any doubt of these propositions, it would not be sufficient to allay the doubt for anyone just to say that he knew them to be true. His objection to Moore was not that the propositions in question were any less certain than Moore had taken them to be but that to say, in the circumstances in which Moore was disposed to say them, such things as 'I know that this is a hand' or 'I know that the earth has existed for many years past' would be a misuse of the expression 'I know'.

Let us first examine the contention that to say that one knows a proposition to be true is not an acceptable method of proving it. We should at least admit that if one is asked for a proof of some proposition which one believes, something more is required than the bare statement that one is convinced of its truth. I think that this applies even to the case of correct descriptions of one's current thoughts or sensations inasmuch as one's ground for accepting them is not one's conviction of their occurrence but the actual occurrence of the experiences which they describe. As for logical axioms, or the application of logical rules of inference, I should be inclined to say not that their proof consisted in one's conviction of their validity, but that there

---

[1] *Philosophical Papers*, p. 146.

came a stage at which a demand for further proof was no longer apposite.

But if one's conviction of the truth of a proposition is not a proof that it is true, why should not there be the same deficiency in one's claim to knowledge? What difference is there between saying that one is certain that something is so and one's saying that one knows it to be so? None at all, according to Wittgenstein, except when 'I know' is meant to mean 'I *can't* be wrong'.[1] But then this claim has to be justified. In Wittgenstein's words, 'It needs to be *shown* that no mistake was possible'.[2] Some objective reason needs to be given for concluding that I must be right.

The seemingly innocuous proposition that if someone knows a proposition to be true he cannot be mistaken about it has been a pitfall for philosophers. They have failed to notice that it expresses no more than a grammatical fact. It is just that the ordinary use of the word 'know', in contexts of this sort, carries the implication that what is known is true. If some proposition which I believed that I knew turns out not to be true, it will follow logically that I did not know it. This is not, however, to say that my state of mind was other than what I took it to be, as though there were a mental attitude of knowledge, as Plato and his numerous followers have mistakenly supposed, which I had confused with the attitude of mere belief. The nature and strength of my conviction might be exactly the same, whether I knew the proposition to be true or whether I mistakenly thought that I knew it. The feeling might be said to be justified in the one case and not in the other, but the difference would then reside not in the quality or strength of the feeling, but in the status of the proposition in question or in the grounds that I might have for accepting it.

It follows that if one wishes to be assured of the truth of some proposition, the fact of someone's saying that he knows it to be true will not meet the purpose unless one has some good reason for believing what he says. Even if we take his honesty for granted, we have to be satisfied both that he has been in a position to acquire the information in question and that it is a genuine item of knowledge. If we are not satisfied on one or other of these counts, we shall be disposed

---

[1] *On Certainty*, para. 8.
[2] ibid., 15.

to ask him how he knows what he has told us or what grounds there are for holding it to be true. In the more common case, in which we are less concerned with his standing as an informant than with the reliability of the information which he professes to be giving us, we shall be asking him for a measure of proof that what he says he knows is really so.

One obvious way in which this demand could be met would be by his supplying us with evidence which gave strong enough support to the proposition concerned, where the evidence consisted of one or more propositions which were themselves equipped with adequate support. However, if these propositions had in their turn to be supported by further propositions for which we had to be supplied with adequate grounds, we should be confronted with an infinite regress. To put a stop to the regress, we must at some point come to propositions which are acceptable in their own right. As we saw not long ago, these might be propositions of logic or records of one's current experience. They would owe their security, not to the support of other propositions but to their own content or to the conditions under which they were expressed.

Wittgenstein does not dispute our need to arrive at propositions which are acceptable in their own right. On the contrary, he treats Moore's examples as being propositions of this sort. What he does deny is that we can legitimately speak of such propositions as being known to be true. Following the same line of reasoning as he had employed in dismissing the possibility of one's having knowledge of one's current sensations, he concludes that when someone like Moore says 'I *know*, I am not just surmising, that here is my hand', he is expressing not an ordinary empirical proposition but 'a proposition of grammar', just as he would be expressing a proposition of grammar if he were to say 'I know, I am not just surmising, that I am seeing red'. But then, Wittgenstein continues, 'If "I know etc" is conceived as a grammatical proposition of course the "I" cannot be important. And it properly means "There is no such thing as a doubt in the case" or "The expression 'I do not know' makes no sense in this case". And of course it follows from this that "I *know*" makes no sense either.'[1]

I have already stated my objection to this whole course of argument.

[1] *On Certainty*, 57 and 58.

I have conceded that it may nearly always be pointless and possibly misleading for me to say such things as 'I know that I am seeing red' or 'I know that these are my hands', but I have tried to show that this in no way entails that what I am saying in these cases is not empirically true.

If statements of these sorts are very often true, does it follow that what one knows is certain? The question presents no problem if, like Moore, we use the word 'certain' in such a way that 'knowing' and 'knowing for certain' are equivalent; and I am not suggesting that this use is incorrect. There are, however, other uses which make the question worth posing. For instance, we might derive from Wittgenstein's restrictions upon knowledge, the proposal that a proposition should be said to be certain only if one could not be mistaken in thinking it true. The point here would be that while knowing excluded, by definition, the fact of error, it did not exclude its possibility. As I have already suggested, the only propositions which might reasonably be held to satisfy this more stringent condition are some that describe one's current experiences and even this claim has been contested. If I do not explore this question further, it is partly because I am hesitant about the answer to it, partly that it does not figure in the future course of our discussion. The only point, in connexion with it, that I now wish to make is that to say of a proposition that one cannot be mistaken in accepting it is not the same as saying that it cannot possibly be false. Let us grant that there are propositions, such as those of logic and mathematics, which are necessarily true. This excludes the possibility of their being false, but not the possibility of our holding a mistaken belief in their truth or falsehood. Notoriously, one can go astray in logic. Conversely, if it is a fact that there are records of immediate experience with regard to which the owner of the experience cannot be mistaken, it does not follow that these propositions are necessary in themselves. They would owe their immunity to the circumstances in which they were believed, and they would bestow their privilege only on a single person and then only for a very short time.

There is also a legitimate use of the word 'certain', perhaps most common among philosophers, according to which certainty is a matter of degree. For instance, a philosopher who does not deny the truth of the proposition that there are trees in his garden, or even deny that he knows this proposition to be true, may still wish to say that it is less certain than some proposition which records his recurrent visual or tactual sensations, whether or not he treats such records as infallible. His reason for assigning a lesser degree of certainty to the proposition about the trees, even though he is quite happy to say that he knows it to be true, will be that simply by claiming more it runs the greater risk of being false. My estimates of the colours which are exemplified in my present visual field may still be true even though I am dreaming or hallucinated. They may still be true even though the interpretations which I put upon my visual data are not corroborated by the tactual data which they would lead me to expect, or by the reports which I receive from other observers. This does not apply, however, to such a proposition as that there are trees in my garden. It is true that I accept it, on the basis of what I think I see, or remember, without looking for any further evidence. I take it for granted that the necessary corroboration would be forthcoming. Even so my present experience does not guarantee that it would be forthcoming, and if it were discovered not to be, I should have reason to conclude that I had been mistaken. This is what has made philosophers like Russell assert that no proposition which implies the existence of a physical object is altogether certain. What they have had in mind is that no such proposition ever logically follows from any set of propositions which merely record the content of one's current sense-experience.

I do not say that this philosophical sense of certainty is deviant, but it may be misleading. Its employment in the present context may be thought to carry the further implication that propositions which imply the existence of physical objects cannot be known to be true, that they all of them are seriously open to doubt, and this would not be a valid inference. Not but what it was a conclusion that Russell himself accepted, at least during the periods when he looked upon physical objects as the external causes of our percepts. Though he considered that the character of our percepts gave us some good reason to believe in the existence of such external causes, he held it to be a genuine possibility that they did not exist.

Rather than accept this conclusion, most contemporary philosophers would argue either that it did not follow from the causal theory of perception, or, if they believed that it did follow, regard this as a decisive argument against the theory. But need they be right? If our belief in the physical world is sacrosanct, what makes it so?

Wittgenstein's answer to this is that it is not an ordinary factual belief but rather part of the frame of reference within which the truth or falsehood of our factual beliefs is assessed. As he puts it:

> All testing, all confirmation and disconfirmation of a hypothesis takes place already within a system. And this system is not a more or less arbitrary and doubtful point of departure for all our arguments: no, it belongs to the essence of what we call an argument. The system is not so much the point of departure, as the element in which arguments have their life.[1]

The system is not, indeed, entirely sacrosanct, since it is susceptible of change, but its propositions can be said to be immune from doubt, in the sense that, so long as they hold their place in the system, it does not occur to us to doubt them. 'What prevents me', asks Wittgenstein, 'from supposing that this table either vanishes or alters its shape and colour when no one is observing it, and then when someone looks at it again changes back to its old condition? – "But who is going to suppose such a thing!" – one would feel like saying.'[2] 'Here we see', he continues, 'that the idea of "agreement with reality" does not have any clear application.'[3] What I take him to be suggesting is that it is only under cover of certain assumptions that the notion of agreement with reality comes into play. These assumptions themselves neither agree nor disagree with reality. They determine the nature of the reality with which agreement is sought.

How far do they extend? This is not a simple question because the system which they combine to constitute is not clearly defined. Wittgenstein speaks of it as an inherited world-picture and of its propositions as being 'part of a kind of mythology'.[4] 'It might be imagined,' he says,

> that some propositions, of the form of empirical propositions, were hardened and functioned as channels for such empirical propositions as were not hardened but fluid: and that this relation altered with time, in that fluid propositions hardened, and hard ones became fluid.

[1] *On Certainty*, para. 105.
[2] ibid., 214.
[3] ibid., 215.
[4] ibid., 95.

The mythology may change back into a state of flux, the river-bed of thoughts may shift. But I distinguish between the movement of the waters on the river-bed and the shift of the bed itself; though there is not a sharp division of the one from the other.

But if someone were to say 'So logic too is an empirical science', he would be wrong. Yet this is right: the same proposition may get treated at one time as something to test by experience, at another as a rule of testing.[1]

The point of this last remark is that a rule of testing is not vulnerable to empirical refutation. In this respect it is assimilated to a necessary proposition. We have, indeed, noted that to say that a proposition is necessary is not to exclude the possibility of our being mistaken about its truth. What is more to the point, however, in the present context, is that we have also noted that if we are in doubt about the validity of our deductive reasoning, there is finally nothing else for us to rely on than our impression that we are following the proper rules. The suggestion that we are in error remains a logical possibility, but there comes a point at which we do not take it seriously. If someone were seriously to regard all our calculations as uncertain, we might think that he was mad, or perhaps only that he was very different from ourselves. 'We rely on calculations, he doesn't; we are sure, he isn't.'[2] I suppose that we should react in this fashion to someone who failed to rely on memory or induction in at all the same way as we do ourselves.

So far as the proceeds of induction go, there is no clear distinction, but at most a difference of degree, between the propositions that sustain Moore's common-sense view of the world and those that we derive from science. Thus, one of Wittgenstein's examples of a proposition which might be said to be certain is the proposition that water boils at about 100 degrees Centigrade. It would, as he says, be accepted unconditionally in a court of law. Even so, the place which such a proposition occupies in our scheme of thought is not entirely secure. If it did come to grief we should not feel that the order of nature had been overturned. Indeed, Wittgenstein himself comes near to acknowledging this:

[1] *On Certainty*, 96–8
[2] ibid., 217.

If I now say 'I know that the water in the kettle on the gas-flame will not freeze but boil', I seem to be as justified in this 'I know' as I am in *any*. 'If I know anything I know *this*.' – Or do I know with still *greater* certainty that the person opposite me is my old friend so-and-so? And how does that compare with the proposition that I am seeing with two *eyes* and shall see them if I look in the glass? – I don't know confidently what I am to answer here. – But still there is a difference between the cases. If the water over the gas freezes, of course I shall be astonished as can be, but I shall assume some factor I don't know of, and perhaps leave the matter to physicists to judge. But what could make me doubt whether this person here is N.N., whom I have known for years? Here a doubt would seem to drag everything with it and plunge it into chaos.[1]

It would, indeed, be astonishing if the water froze, but we have learned to be surprised by science and its applications. Wittgenstein himself unwittingly provides us with a good example since he declared, not unreasonably at the time at which he was writing, 'If we are thinking within our system, then it is certain that no one has ever been on the moon. Not merely is nothing of the sort ever seriously reported to us by reasonable people, but our whole system of physics forbids us to believe it.'[2] How quickly does this system change, and how readily we accept the consequences. Increasingly science is re-garded by the layman as a form of magic with the unhappy result that occult theories and practices, however full of gibberish, are treated as genuine rivals to it. If a measure of certainty is thoroughgoing accept-ance, in a way which requires not only that one assents to a theory but that one rejects beliefs with which it is incompatible, then scientific theories are not so very certain.

How does the matter stand with the common-sense view of the world? Its propositions appear to be more solidly entrenched, at least if we accede to Wittgenstein's requirements that doubt of them be serious and that it be capable of being resolved. Reverting to Moore's example, should we not agree with Wittgenstein that 'The fact that I use the word "hand" and all the other words in my sentence without a second thought, indeed that I should stand before the abyss if I

[1] ibid., 613.
[2] ibid., 108.

wanted so much as to try doubting their meanings – shews that absence of doubt belongs to the essence of the language-game, that the question, "How do I know?" drags out the language-game, or else does away with it'.[1]

This insertion of Moore's example into a language-game is a sign of Wittgenstein's awareness of the peculiarity of philosophical scepticism. I think he realized that the sceptic might be attempting something more radical than making us more cautious about assuming that we know our own names, or that we are using colour-words correctly, or that we were not born yesterday, or that we see with our eyes, or that in normal circumstances we can identify our hands. For instance, a follower of Berkeley, who denies that there are physical objects, is not suggesting that the criteria which we use for determining the existence of such things as trees, or stars, or tables, or human bodies will not continue to be satisfied. He does not suppose that his own experiences are generically unlike those of other people, or that they will be radically different in the future from what they have been in the past. His peculiarity is that he wishes to interpret the evidence in a different fashion. He refuses to make the assumption that anything other than a spiritual substance is capable of existing unperceived.

But then is he not simply wrong on a question of empirical fact? If propositions of the sort that Moore lists in his defence of common sense are true in very many cases, surely it follows that a great many things which are not spiritual substances can exist without being perceived: all the physical objects on Moore's list, for example, and countless others besides. It is true that Berkeley thought it possible to maintain both that there were trees and stars and tables and human bodies and so forth and that there were no such things as physical objects, but is it not obvious that he was mistaken? Surely if the words 'tree' and 'table' and all the rest of them are given their ordinary meanings his position was self-contradictory?

The answer to this is that such a position would indeed have been self-contradictory if the denial of the existence of physical objects had been put forward under the currency of a common-sense theory, which provided for their existence. But this treatment of his views fails to do Berkeley justice. It is true that he himself fostered the misunderstanding

---

[1] *On Certainty*, 370.

by his claim to be protecting common sense against the false sophistication of materialist philosophy. His reason for taking this stance was to accommodate our ordinary perceptual judgements to his philosophical conscience in a way that allowed them to be true, and so incidentally to protect himself against the use of such weapons as Moore wielded. This is a respectable procedure, but not a vindication of common sense. If the common-sense view of the world is supposed to be consistent with what the ordinary man believes that he is doing when he makes perceptual judgements, Berkeley was mistaken in casting himself as its champion. So far from championing the common-sense view, he was seeking to overthrow it. His contention was not that the existence of things, other than minds, at times when they were not perceived, was a possibility that happened not to be realized but that it ought not to be admitted as a possibility. He opted for a radically different way of interpreting experiences, in which this realistic assumption had no place. Consequently, Moore's and Wittgenstein's certainties do not touch him.

Since Wittgenstein uses Moore's claims to knowledge as a springboard, it is worth taking a closer look at what they amounted to. The reason why there is room for doubt here is that while Moore was wholly certain of the truth of the propositions which he listed he was not at all certain of their correct analysis. He did not believe that he or anybody else knew whether his seeing his hand consisted in the fact that some sense-datum was identical with part of the surface of his hand, or in the fact that the sense-datum stood in a causal or some other relation to a set of physical particles which were not themselves directly perceptible, or in the fact that the sense-datum was related in such and such ways to other actual and possible sense-data. His admission of this last possibility brings him strangely close to Berkeley, though I cannot envisage his being content with the part that Berkeley allots to spiritual substances, the concept of which he might have agreed with me in finding unintelligible. What matters here is that Moore's championship of common sense is hardly less deceptive than Berkeley's own.

It is ironical that the one thing Moore took to be certain in the analysis of perception was that in expressing a proposition like 'This is a human hand' one was saying something about a sense-datum, whereas other philosophers, including Wittgenstein, who have been equally certain of the truth of Moore's examples, have denied that sense-data come into it at all. Not only that but Wittgenstein at least, as we have seen, denied that such propositions required analysis. If all that he meant by this was that they were intelligible as they stood, we need not take issue with him. If, on the other hand, he meant that they offered no call for elucidation, he was surely wrong. For instance, there is a long-standing problem with regard to the relation of common-sense propositions about physical objects to the propositions which figure in scientific theories. Are scientific particles, like electrons and neutrons, literally parts of the objects which we see? We have noted that at one stage Wittgenstein declared that they were not. If we accept this denial, do we regard the particles as logical fictions, which we employ as explanatory tools for linking our observations? Or do we allow them an objective physical existence which we deny to the sensibly qualified objects of common sense? Thus Russell notoriously came to hold that 'The table as a physical object, consisting of electrons, positrons and neutrons, lives outside my experience, and if there is a space which contains both it and my perceptual space, then in that space the table must be wholly external to my perceptual space.'[1] I am not suggesting that Russell's view is correct. On the contrary, I think that there are insuperable objections to any theory which puts the occupants of physical space beyond the reach of our observation. But at least Russell believes himself to be tackling a problem which has a correct solution. If we limit ourselves to saying that my acceptance of the proposition that there is a table in front of me is, in my present circumstances, an obligatory move in the language-game that we ordinarily play, then not only do we invite questions about the relations of this game to others that might be playable; we also leave room for differences of opinion as to what the game that we do play actually is.

I have reverted to Wittgenstein's vehicle of a language-game, but we need to consider how far it can carry us. We do indeed sometimes modify our concepts in something like the way in which we alter the rules of games, but in fairness to Wittgenstein we have to allow that many of his examples point to the weaknesses of the analogy. If we adhere to it, we should be aware that the language-game in everyday

---

[1] *Human Knowledge: Its Scope and Limits*, p. 236.

use is one that is played before its rules are codified. This may be part of the point that Wittgenstein was making when he remarked:

> You must bear in mind that the language-game is so to say something unpredictable. I mean: it is not based on grounds. It is not reasonable (or unreasonable).
> It is there – like our life.[1]

Earlier he had said:

> Giving grounds, however, justifying the evidence, comes to an end; – but the end is not certain propositions' striking us immediately as true, i.e. it is not a kind of *seeing* on our part; it is our *acting*, which lies at the bottom of the language-game.[2]

And also:

> Children do not learn that books exist, that armchairs exist, etc. etc., – they learn to fetch books, sit in armchairs, etc. etc.[3]

In these passages I detect an echo not only of the identification of the meaning of a sentence with its use, but of that of its use with the method of verifying the proposition which it serves to express. As the pragmatists, like Peirce and C.I. Lewis, whom Wittgenstein increasingly came to resemble, insisted, we move with a certain freedom between two boundaries; set, on the one side by our theories, on the other by the nature of things. The trouble is that the boundaries are not sharply separated. Our theories have to be adjusted to fit the facts, but the facts are not given to us wholly independently of the fashion in which we describe them. Contemporary philosophy oscillates between realism and irrealism according as it lays the greater stress upon fact or theory. In spite of his declared opposition to theorizing within philosophy, I am inclined to rank Wittgenstein with the irrealists. I take the impossibility of there being any cognitive process which would permit the prising of the world off language as being a constant factor throughout the vagaries of Wittgenstein's thought. To whatever extent it runs through Schopenhauer, this establishes a link between his work and the still more esoteric philosophy of Immanuel Kant.

[1] ·*On Certainty*, para. 559.
[2] ibid., 204.
[3] ibid., 476.

10

WITTGENSTEIN'S INFLUENCE

The most eminent philosophers at Cambridge, when Wittgenstein went there as a pupil in 1912, were Bertrand Russell and G. E. Moore, and we have already seen how deeply he impressed them both. This was due not only to his manifest aptitude for philosophy but also to the strength of his personality. How great an influence did he exert upon their philosophical views? In Moore's case I believe the answer to be that he exerted hardly any influence at all. We have, indeed, seen that Moore deferred to him, to the extent of visiting him in Norway in 1914 and taking notes at his dictation, and attending and taking notes at his lectures and discussion classes at Cambridge over a period of three years in the early Thirties, besides acknowledging Wittgenstein's superiority in the passage which I have already quoted from the autobiography which he supplied in 1942 for *The Philosophy of G.E. Moore*[1] and there also owning to a suspicion that what was required for the solution of philosophical problems was a method quite different from any that he himself had ever used, one that Wittgenstein used successfully but Moore did not understand clearly enough to use himself. Nevertheless the facts remain that he stayed loyal to the methods which he had developed independently of Wittgenstein, that he made no attempt to imitate Wittgenstein's methods at any stage or to borrow anything of moment from his views, and that the only substantial reference to Wittgenstein which occurs in Moore's *Common-Place Book*, covering the period from 1919 to 1953, is a criticism of the account of truth-functions that Wittgenstein had given in the *Tractatus*. All that we are left with is the admission in Moore's autobiography that his divergences from Wittgenstein had made him less confi-

[1] See p. 12.

dent than he might otherwise have been of the truth of his own philosophical opinions.

Betrand Russell's case is more complicated. Wittgenstein's influence over him was almost wholly confined to the years 1912-13, when he was nominally Russell's pupil, but while it lasted it was very strong. We have already seen that his criticism dissuaded Russell from completing a book on the theory of knowledge on which Russell was engaged in 1913. The lectures entitled *Our Knowledge of the External World* which Russell did deliver and publish in 1914 owed more to Alfred North Whitehead, his collaborator on *Principia Mathematica*, than they did to Wittgenstein, but he admitted to 'making use of unpublished work by my friend Ludwig Wittgenstein' in advancing the view, which Wittgenstein subsequently expounded in the *Tractatus*, that logical constants like 'or' and 'not' and the operators of generalization perform a purely formal function. Russell makes this point briefly at the close of a passage in which he has been arguing that classes and consequently numbers 'are not things' either, but does not develop it any further, beyond saying that it has a very important bearing on all logic and philosophy.[1]

In several of his works Russell speaks of his having been convinced by Wittgenstein that the propositions of logic are tautologies. He seems to have agreed with Wittgenstein's characterization of a tautology as a proposition which is compatible with every possible distribution of truth and falsehood among atomic propositions. Since this account applies only to propositions which owe their necessity to the operations of logical constants, it gives the notion of tautology a narrower extension than that of analyticity. Russell always accepted the analytic-synthetic distinction and can, I think, be said to have regarded an analytic proposition as one the truth of which depends only on the meaning of the words by which it is expressed. On the other hand, even if we extend the domain of logic so that propositions which are analytic in this sense are allowed to be logically true, Russell rejected Wittgenstein's view that there is no necessity outside logic. A counter-example, which he gives in *An Inquiry into Meaning and Truth*, published in 1940, is the proposition: 'At a given time and in a given visual field, if the colour A is at the place θ,ϕ. no other colour

[1] *Our Knowledge of the External World*, pp. 207-8.

B is at this place.'[1] 'Red and blue', he argues, 'are no more *logically* incompatible than red and round.'[2] Wittgenstein held that they are grammatically incompatible, in a context of this sort, and would have dismissed Russell's proposition as offending against the grammar of colour-terms. Here my sympathies lie with Wittgenstein, though I wish, once again, that his pronouncement had been less oracular.

Russell's greatest debt to Wittgenstein is to be seen in a series of eight lectures entitled 'The Philosophy of Logical Atomism' which he delivered in London early in 1918 and published in *The Monist*, and in an essay 'On Propositions: What they are and how they mean' which appeared in the *Supplementary Proceedings of the Aristotelian Society* in 1919. Both are reprinted in a collection of Russell's essays entitled *Logic and Knowledge*. The lectures foreshadow Wittgenstein's *Tractatus* in maintaining that the world consists of atomic facts, though, unlike Wittgenstein, Russell included negative facts among them, and also committed himself to saying that the 'logical atoms' which made up the facts would some of them be what he called 'particulars' – 'such things as little patches of colour or sounds, momentary things' – and some of them predicates and relations. It was presumably also from Wittgenstein that Russell acquired the pictorial theory of language which he married to a correspondence theory of truth. Thus in the essay 'On Propositions' we find him speaking of 'word-propositions' as meaning 'image-propositions' and of an image-proposition as being true if and only if there is a fact which it resembles. There is no need to go into the ramifications of this theory, as we have already exposed its fundamental flaw.

There is no doubt that Russell greatly admired Wittgenstein's *Tractatus*, though the introduction which he wrote for it is not entirely uncritical. If Wittgenstein objected to it, the reasons may well have been first that Russell represented him as setting out the conditions which would have to be fulfilled by an ideal language, whereas Wittgenstein intended his work to provide a general account of the relation of language to the world, and secondly Russell's suggestion that the awkwardness of Wittgenstein's having to brand his own utterances as nonsensical could be avoided if he allowed there to be a hierarchy of

[1] p. 82.
[2] ibid.

languages, in each of which significant remarks could be made about the structure of its predecessor, this being a possibility which Wittgenstein had given no signs of envisaging and was never willing to accept.

We have seen that Russell was willing to recommend Wittgenstein for a grant from Trinity in 1930 on the basis of a manuscript of which he had read no more than a third. I suspect that he was still judging Wittgenstein on the basis of the *Tractatus*. In the last of his own philosophical works, *My Philosophical Development*, which came out in 1959, Russell spoke of the *Tractatus* as having had 'very considerable influence upon my own thinking'[1] though in fact the influence derived less from the *Tractatus* itself than from the ideas, preliminary to it, which Wittgenstein had expounded to Russell before 1914. Russell went on to say that he did not, in 1959, think that this influence was wholly good, but this slightly adverse judgement may have been coloured by the extremely jaundiced view which we shall see that Russell took of Wittgenstein's *Investigations* and of the philosophical movement which he believed this work to have inspired.

F.P. Ramsey's review of the *Tractatus*, which was published in *Mind* in 1923 and re-issued as an appendix to Ramsey's posthumous *The Foundations of Mathematics*, declared the book to be of extraordinary interest but made damaging criticisms both of its theory of representation and of its treatment of propositional attitudes. He took its chief achievement to be its bringing to light that the essential characteristic of the propositions of logic is that they are tautologies. So far as his own papers went, it was only in those which served the cause of mathematical logic that Ramsey paid respect to Wittgenstein. In his philosophical articles and brilliant, though fragmentary, 'last papers', the pragmatic influence of C.S. Peirce, whose work had come to Ramsey's notice through the publication in 1921 of the selection of essays entitled *Chance, Love and Logic*, was far stronger.

In the decade which succeeded its publication, the *Tractatus* made little mark outside Austria and England and in these countries its influence was not fully felt before the inauguration in 1925 of the Vienna Circle and the vigorous development in England in the early 1930s of the analytical movement in philosophy. It is difficult to estimate how much the Vienna Circle owed to Wittgenstein but its debt

---

[1] p.216.

was certainly increased by the revival of Wittgenstein's interest in philosophy in 1927, which we have already noted, and his conversations with Schlick, Waismann and Carnap. For instance, Waismann's article in an early number of *Erkenntnis* on the subject of probability was a development of what I have treated as a mistaken theory of Wittgenstein's, and Carnap's book *Der Logische Aufbau der Welt* (*The Logical Construction of the World*), which was published in 1928, was a serious endeavour to employ purely logical tools for the erection of a pyramid of concepts, sufficient for the complete description of reality, on the basis of a single person's experience. The enterprise was not successful, though none the less worth attempting, and the choice of the basis not endorsed by Wittgenstein but not at that stage repudiated by him either.

The members of the Circle who were not in personal contact with Wittgenstein, of whom the most conspicuous were Hans Hahn and Otto Neurath, acknowledged their debt to him for what they took to be his discovery that the true propositions of logic are tautologies, though here Gödel may have had his private reservations, and joined with Schlick and Carnap in wholeheartedly endorsing his condemnation of metaphysics and his proposal to replace 'traditional philosophy' by an activity of clarification, directed especially upon scientific concepts. I do not know that any of them other than Neurath explicitly reprobated the hankering after the unsayable which was latent in the *Tractatus*, though Carnap and probably Gödel also were ready to allow wider limits to what could be said, but whether or not they came to be suspicious of Wittgenstein, the members of the Circle as a whole had no indulgence at all for mysticism and accepted at its face value the relegation in the *Tractatus* of metaphysics to the rubbish heap of the nonsensical.

This was certainly true of me. If I remember rightly, it was in 1931, my second year as an undergraduate, that my tutor, Gilbert Ryle, introduced me to the *Tractatus* and it had an immediate and overwhelming effect upon my thinking. Like the members of the Vienna Circle, I had no truck with the pictorial theory of language. Like them, again with the exception of Gödel, I was entirely persuaded that the true propositions of logic and pure mathematics were tautologies or equations, in either case 'saying nothing', that there was no such thing as natural necessity, that metaphysics was strictly nonsensical and that there remained no function for philosophy but the practice of analysis, preferably directed upon the theories and concepts of science. Though the *Tractatus* had been published as long before as 1922, practically no notice had been taken of it at Oxford. Apart from Gilbert Ryle, I believe that few Oxford tutors were even aware of its existence, and after flirting with phenomenology in the 1920s, Ryle had rallied to Russell rather than to Wittgenstein. The paper on the *Tractatus* which I read to the Jowett Society in 1932 may well have been the first exposition of the work at Oxford since its publication ten years before.

Naturally things were different at Cambridge, but even there I doubt if much attention was paid to Wittgenstein's work before his return to Trinity in 1929. G.E. Moore and C.D. Broad went their own ways at all times and R.B. Braithwaite worked closely with Ramsey, whom we have seen to be moving in the direction of pragmatism in the closing years of his short life. Even so, an aura of the *Tractatus*, supplementing the stronger influences of Russell and Moore, is discernible in the vigorous growth of the analytic movement in England in the 1930s, marked by the founding of the journal *Analysis* in 1933, and the publication in 1936 of my *Language, Truth and Logic*, which has survived as a text-book of 'Logical Positivism', a philosophical development for which the *Tractatus* bore some historical responsibility, however little Wittgenstein may have welcomed his association with it. Among the adherents of the analytic movement, whose hostility to metaphysics was mostly less radical than my own, were professors Susan Stebbing and C.A. Mace in London, John Wisdom at Cambridge and his cousin J.O. Wisdom, Margaret Macdonald, Karl Britton, Max Black, who published a detailed commentary on the *Tractatus* as late as 1964, and the original editor of *Analysis*, Austin Duncan-Jones.

During this period, while many of us were still drawing inspiration from the *Tractatus*, Wittgenstein himself, as we have seen, was radically changing his philosophical approach. Owing to his secretiveness, only Schlick and Waismann in Vienna and the narrow circle of Wittgenstein's pupils in Cambridge were equipped to appreciate how far these changes went. The effect on Schlick, who died in 1936, was to consolidate his belief in the principle of verifiability. The effect on Waismann is best seen in the constructivist tenor of his *Einführung in das mathematische Denken (Introduction to Mathematical Thinking)*, which was published in Vienna in 1936 and translated into English in 1951. It would have been more fully apparent, over a wider field, if Wittgenstein had allowed him to complete and publish his *Logik, Sprache, Philosophie*. In much the same way Wittgenstein sought to prevent his Cambridge pupils from publishing any work which might be thought to be derived from his teaching, however humbly they acknowledged their indebtedness to him. I think only Alice Ambrose evaded the ban with an article on the foundations of mathematics which obtained entry into *Mind*, and it led to Wittgenstein's bitterly disowning her.

Wittgenstein could not exact the same subservience from his colleagues, of whom John Wisdom was the only one to display any marked signs of his influence. This was freely admitted by Wisdom but not by Wittgenstein who quarrelled with me in 1946 for suggesting, in an article and a broadcast, that Wisdom's published views were indicative of his own. What chiefly offended him was the suggestion that his philosophical technique bore any close resemblance to psycho-analysis, a kinship which Wisdom was disposed to claim for his own work. Since Wisdom, like his cousin J.O. Wisdom, who shocked philosophers by connecting Berkeley's hostility to materialism with the workings of his digestion, was well versed in the literature of psycho-analysis, his claim may have been well founded. So far as I am concerned, its acceptance would not assist me in the understanding either of Wisdom's or of Wittgenstein's work. Neither am I equipped to measure Wisdom's debt to Wittgenstein, though I suspect it to be smaller than Wisdom's tributes to Wittgenstein might lead his readers to suppose. A point which I do think worth making is that I attach a greater value to Wisdom's *Other Minds* than to the writings of Wittgenstein in what I have called his period of transition. The two are alike in seeing the problems of philosophy in general, and that of one's knowledge of other minds in particular, as problems to be dissolved, but Wisdom's choice of examples is at least equally imaginative and his use of the method of dialogue sets the issues out more clearly. Where Wittgenstein's remarks are suggestive, Wisdom's characters argue.

In his collection of essays *Paradox and Discovery*, published in 1964, Wisdom devotes one of them to the views that Wittgenstein was expressing during the years 1934-7, another to 'A feature of Wittgenstein's technique', and a third, in which Wittgenstein barely figures, to a comparison of his methods with those of Moore and C.A. Mace. None of this adds anything of significance to what we have already noted about the development of Wittgenstein's thought. The points to which Wisdom draws attention are Wittgenstein's substitution of 'family resemblances' for 'common qualities', his objection to the idea that the meaning of a word is an object, his awareness of the need to discern whether a proposition is being maintained as a logical or an empirical truth, his insistence on the careful examination of particular instances, especially when it is a matter of elucidating what pass for mental acts. Wisdom makes one comment which puzzles me. 'If', he says, 'I were asked to answer, in one sentence, the question "What was Wittgenstein's biggest contribution to philosophy?", I should answer "His asking of the question 'Can one play chess without the queen?' " '[1] The answer to this question seems to me arbitrary, and its profundity escapes me.

Wittgenstein was on good if fairly distant terms with Gilbert Ryle and they used to meet occasionally in the 1930s. I do not know how far they discussed philosophy, though Ryle, like others of us at Oxford, had at least had a glimpse of both the *Blue and Brown Books*, and may have questioned Wittgenstein about them, but there are points of similarity between Ryle's *The Concept of Mind* which was published in 1949 and Wittgenstein's *Investigations* of which the first part we have seen to be complete by 1945. I have no thought of accusing Ryle of plagiarism, but he may have undergone some subconscious influence. The two books are markedly divergent in style but there is some overlapping of content. Indeed, Wittgenstein's dictum that an inner process stands in need of outward criteria could be taken as the guiding principle of Ryle's attack upon 'the ghost in the machine'. In my opinion the attack failed,[2] just as Wittgenstein failed to demolish private languages, but in neither case was the failure total. In their different ways, both philosophers effectively curtailed the empire of the mind.

Bertrand Russell thought very poorly of *The Concept of Mind* and while he does not suggest that Ryle was influenced by Wittgenstein and nowhere mentions J.L. Austin, who more than either Ryle or

---

[1] p. 88.
[2] See my essay 'An Honest Ghost?', reprinted in my *Freedom and Morality*.

Wittgenstein promoted the 'linguistic philosophy' of the 1950s which aroused Russell's contempt, it was Wittgenstein's *Philosophical Investigations* that Russell singled out as dominating 'the British philosophical world' in 1959. Referring to the school which he believed it to have inspired as W II, as opposed to the W I of the *Tractatus*, he said of it in his book *My Philosophical Development* that 'it remains to me completely unintelligible.' He continues:

> Its positive doctrines seem to me trivial and its negative doctrines unfounded. I have not found in Wittgenstein's *Philosophical Investigations* anything that seemed to me interesting and I do not understand why a whole school finds important wisdom in its pages. The earlier Wittgenstein, whom I knew intimately, was a man addicted to passionately intense thinking, profoundly aware of difficult problems of which I, like him, felt the importance, and possessed (or at least so I thought) of true philosophical genius. The late Wittgenstein, on the contrary, seems to have grown tired of serious thinking and to have invented a doctrine which would make such an activity unnecessary. I do not for one moment believe that the doctrine which has these lazy consequences is true. I realize, however, that I have an overpoweringly strong bias against it, for, if it is true, philosophy is, at best, a slight help to lexicographers, and at worst, an idle tea-table amusement.[1]

This is an excessively harsh judgement of the work of what Russell calls Wittgenstein II. Russell had been disappointed by the cool reception given to the last of his major philosophical works, *Human Knowledge: Its Scope and Limits*, which had been published in 1948, and he resented the fact that philosophical fashion in England had come to subordinate his work to that of Wittgenstein and Moore. Contemporary fashion would place him ahead of Moore and less certainly ahead of all of Wittgenstein. In any case, it was not simply a matter of personal pique. Russell did not discriminate between the preoccupation with language which is manifested in Wittgenstein's *Investigations*, the resort to linguistic arguments in which Ryle occasionally indulges in *The Concept of Mind*, and the confinement of philosophy to an examination of ordinary English usage which J.L. Austin succeeded in imposing on most of his juniors at Oxford in the 1950s. A

[1] pp. 216-17.

judgement which treats them as the leaders of a linguistic school, with Wittgenstein's *Investigations* as its principal source, is historically crude. We have seen that Ryle was probably indebted to Wittgenstein but he disliked Austin and was not influenced by him. The fact, which we have noted, that Wittgenstein wrote in 1950 of Oxford as 'a philosophical desert' implies little respect for Ryle. One or two of Austin's papers had been published before Wittgenstein's death but it is unlikely that he read them or that he would have read their successors if his life had been prolonged. If he had read them, he would most probably have disapproved of them, if only on the ground of their suggesting that the careful examination of ordinary usage was a means to the solution of philosophical problems, or in other words that philosophical problems were linguistic problems in disguise. This is clearly at variance with Wittgenstein's final conception of philosophy as posing no problems that are capable of solution, but as being a process of falling into bewilderment by being caught in linguistic traps and escaping from these traps by the better understanding of the actual use of language that works like the *Investigations* provide.

It is this conception of philosophy that accounts, more than anything else, for Russell's hostility to Wittgenstein II and those whom he considers, on the whole unfairly, to belong to that school. The paragraph which succeeds our previous quotation from *My Philosophical Development* begins:

> In common with all philosophers before W II, my fundamental aim has been to understand the world as well as may be, and to separate what may count as knowledge from what must be rejected as unfounded opinion. But for W II I should not have thought it worth while to state this aim, which I should have supposed could be taken for granted. But we are now told that it is not the world that we are to understand but only sentences, and it is assumed that all sentences can count as true except those uttered by philosophers. This, however, is perhaps an overstatement. Adherents of W II are fond of pointing out, as if it were a discovery, that sentences may be interrogative, imperative or optative as well as indicative. This, however, does not take us beyond the realm of sentences.[1]

The remark that it is no discovery that not all sentences are in the

---

[1] ibid., p. 217.

indicative is a mockery of Wittgenstein's frequent reminders in the *Investigations* of the multifarious uses to which language is put. It would not have appeased Russell to be told that this was one of the ways that Wittgenstein chose to distance his later self from the author of the *Tractatus*. The characteristically mischievous attribution to the school of the later Wittgenstein of the assumption that all (indicative) sentences can count as true except those uttered by philosophers is an attack not only on the peculiar conception of philosophy which we have seen to be displayed in the *Investigations* but still more on Wittgenstein's acceptance of everyday language as perfectly in order and the implicit adherence of philosophers like Ryle and Austin to Moore's championship of common sense. In Russell's view, these philosophers were even more at fault than Moore, who at least admitted his ignorance of the way in which common-sense propositions should be analysed, and believed that this ignorance was capable of being remedied, inasmuch as some form of analysis was actually correct. On the other hand, Ryle and Austin appeared to be perfectly at home with naive realism, and we have already found Wittgenstein affirming that mathematics no more needs a foundation than propositions about physical objects need an analysis. We have also seen that his objection to Moore's defence of common sense, so far from implying any doubts about naive realism, was based on the belief that Moore's propositions were so firmly entrenched that it was a mistake, by seeking to defend them, to admit even the possibility of their being vulnerable. All this was heresy to Russell who dismissed common sense as the metaphysics of savages and thought that naive realism was scientifically untenable. 'Naive realism', he says, in a well-known passage of his *An Inquiry into Meaning and Truth*, 'leads to physics, and physics, if true, shows that naive realism is false. Therefore, naive realism, if true, is false; therefore, it is false.'[1]

This argument is a little too simple as it stands. Physics offers us an explanation of the ways in which physical objects appear to us and it does so in terms of particles which lack the perceptible properties which we attribute to the objects of common sense. Even so, it does not obviously follow that our beliefs that grass is green, that stones are hard and that snow is cold, to take three of Russell's examples,

[1] p. 15.

are not literally true. What does follow is that if we are to uphold the claims of common sense, without discounting those of physics, we need to interpret them both in a manner that shows them not to be in conflict; and the questions whether this is possible, and if so how it is to be effected, fall into the province of philosophical analysis. To exclude such questions by fiat as Wittgenstein and the devotees of ordinary usage may be said to have done is to break with a long-established philosophical tradition of which Russell himself in the twentieth century has been the most eminent representative.

In saying that Wittgenstein seemed to have grown tired of serious thinking, Russell was certainly unfair to him. There was next to no touch of frivolity in Wittgenstein's character, and there are many witnesses to the intensity with which he conducted his philosophical classes. His absorption in philosophy until the very end of his life is confirmed by the vast quantity and variety of more or less well-ordered notes which it fell to his executors to assemble and publish. If Russell's charge is to be accorded any substance it has to be seen as directed not against Wittgenstein's practice but against the conception of philosophy which he seemed to be upholding. Merely to describe how our ordinary language actually functions might well appear to Russell as not requiring any great intellectual effort.

There is a misunderstanding here for which Wittgenstein himself was largely responsible. His repeated preference for description over explanation and the avoidance of theory which he claimed to practise and enjoined upon his readers are not characteristic of his actual procedure at any stage of his development, including that of the *Investigations*. That his explanations are runic does not reduce them to descriptions: his theories do not cease to be such by being covertly set out. Wittgenstein's whole flirtation with behaviourism is an attempt, the success of which is open to question, to explain the operations of the mind. His suggestion that philosophy leaves everything as it was; more obviously his attempt to outlaw private languages, are both of them embodiments of philosophical theories. One of my principal objects has been to show that these theories are false.

Russell's complaint that the school of Wittgenstein II did not venture beyond sentences was explicitly directed not against the *Investigations* nor even against the Oxford linguistic philosophers but against a phase of logical positivism in which some of its adherents, notably Carnap,

Neurath and Hempel, maintained that sentences could be compared only with other sentences: it was metaphysical to talk of comparing sentences with facts. They were thereby forced into accepting a coherence theory of truth. To the obvious objection that many incompatible systems could each be internally coherent, Carnap replied that the true one was that which was accepted by the scientists of our culture circle. Russell's retort to this was that merely finding the utterances of such persons printed on a page was no guarantee of their truth. I made the more telling objection, or perhaps what comes down to the same objection in a more telling fashion, by pointing out that each one of the competing systems of sentences might consistently contain the sentence that it alone was accepted by contemporary scientists. What Carnap needed to maintain was that only one of the systems was so accepted in fact. Even here it might be argued that since contemporary scientists are not infallible, their acceptance of a system is not a guarantee of its truth, but that was not the point of my objection. My point was rather that the coherence theory comes to grief if it needs to be buttressed by an appeal to fact of any kind. If the beliefs of contemporary scientists can be a matter of fact, then there can be matters of fact of many other sorts, whether more or less recondite; as of course there obviously are.

Carnap and his friends were rescued from the trap in which they had ensnared themselves by the promulgation at the Paris congress of the Vienna Circle in 1935 of a simplified version of Alfred Tarski's theory of truth, which convinced those present at the congress that semantics was respectable. What was important, in this regard, was not the actual definition of truth which Tarski devised, in terms of the concept of fulfilment, for a particular formal language, but the criterion of adequacy which he imposed on any definition of truth with respect to any language. This was that the definition should entail a statement of the truth-conditions for each of the sentences of the language in question, where the formulation of the truth-conditions bridged the quotation or structural description of a sentence and its factual assertion. As it happens, Tarski denied the possibility of defining truth for a natural language, like English, in a way that satisfied his condition of adequacy. He thought that any attempt at such a definition would fall foul of the paradox of the liar, whereby a statement is made to say of itself that it is false. Many subsequent philosophers, who have sought to build upon Tarski's foundations, have felt free to ignore this warning, and I am not going to broach the question whether they are justified. What matters in the present context is that Tarski provided a ground for saying that sentences could be compared with facts.

Considering that the main burden of Wittgenstein's *Tractatus* was the problem of relating language to fact, I find it strange that Wittgenstein paid no attention to Tarski's work. Not that he ever relapsed into holding a coherence theory of truth. He remained loyal to the theory which we have already attributed to him; the so-called redundancy theory, according to which the ascription of truth to a proposition is tantamount to affirming it and the ascription of falsehood is tantamount to denying it.

Wittgenstein's failure to treat semantics systematically does not imprison him in syntax, as Russell unfairly assumed that it must. His language-games are not merely games with words. His case is well put by J.L. Austin, who was defending his own procedure against a similar charge: 'When we examine what we should say when, what words we should use in what situations, we are looking again not *merely* at words (or "meanings" whatever they may be) but also at the realities we use the words to talk about: we are using a sharpened awareness of words to sharpen our perception of, though not as the final arbiter of, the phenomena.'[1]

Though I am allowing Austin here to speak for Wittgenstein, there are subtle differences in their technique. Austin is the more inclined to make straightforwardly grammatical points such as his denial that the words 'voluntarily' and 'involuntarily' are opposed 'in the obvious sort of way that they are made to be in philosophy or jurisprudence'. 'The "opposite", or rather "opposite" of "voluntary", might,' he says, 'be "under constraint of some sort, duress or obligation or influence",' remarking in a footnote that 'When I sign a cheque in the normal way, I do *not* do so *either* "voluntarily" *or* "under constraint".' 'The opposite of "involuntarily" might be "deliberately" or "on purpose" or the like.'[2] Wittgenstein also gives examples of voluntary and involuntary actions but not in such detail. For all his talk of grammar, one is left

[1] J.L. Austin, *Philosophical Papers*, p. 130.
[2] ibid., p. 139.

with the impression that he is not so greatly interested in grammatical nuances. To return to one of his examples occurring in both the *Brown Book* and the *Investigations*, when he presents us with the English word 'reading', or strictly speaking, the German word '*lesen*', he does not enumerate the many different contexts in which the word is used and show us how to discriminate between them. We are not taken through the German equivalents of 'lip-reading', or 'reading fortunes', or 'reading between the lines'. We are asked rather to consider what happens when someone, who has learned to read his native language, reads a newspaper; how his eye passes along the printed words, how he may or may not say them out loud, how he may or may not take in their shapes as wholes, how he may or may not attend to what he reads, and then we are asked to compare this case with that of a beginner who laboriously spells words out; and this case again with that of a person who pretends to read a passage which he has learned by heart; there is talk also of creatures that are used as reading-machines and persons under the influence of drugs. Several pages are devoted to this subject in the *Investigations*,[1] and the conclusion of them all is that there is no one feature that occurs in all cases of reading. We are supposed also to be relieved of the temptation to take reading as consisting in a special conscious activity of mind.

These examples, and many others that I could give, indicate a significant difference of approach between the two so-called linguistic philosophers. Austin assembles data about the use of a word or the use of a cluster of related words and is often content to mark distinctions without drawing any general conclusions from them. A reproach which he brings against philosophers is that they are too ready to generalize on the basis of insufficient evidence. Wittgenstein, though he claims to be opposed to theorizing in philosophy, almost always makes his data point a moral. Repeatedly, as in the example which we have just been considering, the moral is that we must be cautious in our invocation of acts of consciousness and also that in examining the extension of what appears to be a single concept we must often expect to find family resemblances among its various instances rather than a common quality.

What influence have these and the other main theses of the *Investiga-*

---

[1] *Investigations*, paras 156–71, and see above, pp. 55–6.

tions had? We have noted that both in what I have called his inter-mediate period and in his later work Wittgenstein was concerned to destroy the assumptions which underlay the *Tractatus*, and in this I think that he has been successful. There has been no revival of the belief in a pictorial theory of language and at least a diminution of the belief in logical atomism. I speak of a diminution because I myself am still disposed to think of the world as a four-dimensional continuum consisting of observable states of affairs with no necessary connections between them. I believe that something the same is true of Professor Quine though he takes the content of any portion of space-time to be a physical object, and for the sake of mathematics includes abstract classes in his enumeration of what there is. To allow him any attach-ment to logical atomism might seem to run counter to the so-called holism of which he is thought to be one of the principal exponents. But, so far as I understand it, the basis of this holism is just that the components of our theories face experience as a body. If a theory comes to grief we have a choice of ways in which to patch it up. This does not exclude the view that true observation sentences are logically independent of one another. What makes me doubtful about linking Quine, even as loosely as I have, with the inheritance of logical atom-ism is his theory of meaning, which leaves it uncertain whether his observation sentences refer to definite states of affairs.

One thing that has gone by the board is the belief in the possibility of thoroughgoing reduction; in particular, the reduction of statements about physical matters of fact to statements about sense-data. Even I, who am one of the few philosophers still to believe that talk of sensory qualities is legitimate and that the reference to them is helpful to the analysis of perception, no longer adhere to the classic doctrine of phenomenalism, according to which every physical statement can be reformulated in their terms; the most I should claim is that they furnish a basis with respect to which our common-sense conception of physical objects can be exhibited as a theory. If even moderate claims of this sort are out of favour, as I fear they are, I suppose that the chief responsibility lies with Ryle and Austin but Wittgenstein also played a part. I myself have argued that sense qualia should not be identified from the outset as private entities, but this is how they have most commonly been treated and consequently their use as elements in a theory of perception, or indeed in a theory of any kind, has been thought by many philosophers to be forbidden by Wittgenstein's argument against the possibility of private languages. I believe that I have shown this argument to be invalid, but this is not a belief that is so far very widely shared.

A point of more general importance is that Wittgenstein was very largely responsible for diverting Western philosophy from a course which it had steadily pursued from Descartes to Russell. There had been notable exceptions, in the persons of such metaphysicians as Spinoza and Nietzsche, but broadly speaking, the dominant tradition, inaugurated by Descartes, was one that assigned a central role to the theory of knowledge. We have seen that it would not be true to say that Wittgenstein entirely ignored the theory of knowledge: his private-language argument bears on it and he was seriously occupied, especially in *The Blue Book*, with the problem of one's knowledge of other minds. Nevertheless we have also seen that in his principal works, the *Tractatus* and the *Investigations*, in their very different ways, and conspicuously in his *Remarks on the Philosophy of Psychology*, the theory of knowledge is subordinated to the study of meaning.

It could be argued that the study of meaning has always been a principal feature of the analytical movement, which may be held to have originated in the works of Russell and Moore at the beginning of this century and to have encompassed Wittgenstein. This is undoubtedly true but it is also true that Russell and Moore, as well as the analysts of the 1930s, like Susan Stebbing, Richard Braithwaite and John Wisdom, enlisted the study of meaning in the cause of the assessment of beliefs. The will-o'-the-wisp of phenomenalist reduction was sought as a guarantee of respectability. The logical positivists wasted no time in trying to prove their principle of verifiability, in whatever form they held it. Having used it as a weapon to dispose of metaphysics they hoped to put it at the service of the natural and the social sciences, a distinction which they anyhow intended to obliterate. They were not interested in meaning for its own sake.

Wittgenstein was and so have many other philosophers been in the years that have passed since his death. The theory of knowledge has not been altogether abandoned but it has faded into the background. What is curious is how little the attempts made to develop theories of meaning appear to owe to Wittgenstein as a precursor. Michael Dummett is ready enough to quote Wittgenstein but looks at him always in the light of Frege. Quine barely notices the *Investigations*. Donald Davidson tries to build on Tarski's treatment of truth. Other American philosophers, like Chomsky and Fodor, adopt a scientific approach. To the extent that they are worth mentioning in this company, such French philosophers as Foucault and Derrida have busied themselves with sociology or with literary criticism.

Considering the strength of his personality and his total commitment to his own conception of philosophy, one might have expected Wittgenstein to found an important school of philosophers at Cambridge, operating to a greater or lesser extent in his own image. If this has not come about, the main responsibility lies with Wittgenstein himself. He was not averse from having disciples but he tended to overawe them, thereby curtailing their powers of independent thought, and in certain cases at least he discouraged them from the pursuit of philosophy as an academic career. Regarding John Wisdom as predominantly his own man, and anyhow one who owed as much to Moore as to Wittgenstein, I can think of no one but Elizabeth Anscombe who has made an original contribution to philosophy on the basis of Wittgenstein's teaching. Von Wright is an excellent philosopher, and a person whom Wittgenstein trusted, but his philosophy seems to me far removed from Wittgenstein's. If any Cambridge influence is detectable in it, it is rather that of C.D. Broad.

In so far as the tendency of philosophy in recent years, especially in the United States, has been to effect a rapprochement with the natural sciences, it may be said to have moved away from Wittgenstein. It is true that the *Tractatus* rendered homage to science by leaving it mistress of all that could be said, and true also that members of the Vienna Circle, most notably Rudolf Carnap, ascribed to Wittgenstein a large measure of responsibility for their view that the only creditable future for philosophy lay in its becoming what Carnap called the logic of science. Nevertheless, as I hope that my tracing of his development has shown, Wittgenstein increasingly came to see science as inimical to philosophy. To put it more accurately, he thought that the prestige of science misled philosophers into fabricating explanations, whereas what was needed was an assortment of careful descriptions. He also blamed it for their failure to distinguish between conceptual and empirical questions. He might indeed have taken more pains to show that this is not a clear-cut distinction, and allowed that it is one that arises within the domain of science itself.

There is, however, another respect in which Wittgenstein, in his later work, so far from being at odds with contemporary fashion, may be said to have been in the forefront of it, and that is in the concessions which he makes to relativity: what might in current jargon be called his irrealism. We have seen that this comes out most strongly in his treatment of mathematics, but it is also to be seen in the use of his concept of language-games, and in his assessment of linguistic practices, no longer as portrayals of a single independent reality, but in terms of the part that they play in different forms of human life.

The position of irrealism has been most forcibly summarized by Nelson Goodman, a philosopher whose systematic treatment of philosophy in his earlier work puts him almost wholly at variance with the later Wittgenstein but one who narrows the gap in his recent book entitled *Ways of Worldmaking*. In the course of paying tribute to the philosopher Ernst Cassirer, he finds occasion to refer to the two apparently conflicting statements 'The Sun always moves' and 'The Sun never moves', assigning them to different frames of reference. 'Frames of reference, though,' he says, 'seems to belong less to what is described than to systems of description: and each of the two statements relates what is described to such a system. If I ask about the world, you can offer to tell me how it is under one or more frames of reference, but if I insist that you tell me how it is apart from all frames, what can you say? We are confined to ways of describing whatever is described. Our universe, so to speak, consists of these ways rather than of a world or of worlds.'[1]

On this basis Goodman develops a theory of 'world-versions', which strikes me as being a close counterpart of Wittgenstein's language-games. World-versions may be right or wrong, though it is not made clear, to me at least, how this is determined, but when two such versions are internally right, even though they may appear incompatible, there is no deciding between them. Perception is not the final arbiter since it has been experimentally proved that what we might suppose to be given in perception is very much the outcome of our own construction.

[1] pp. 2-3.

I do not know whether Wittgenstein would have gone to these lengths, but a study of the *Investigations* favours the answer that he would. On the other hand, the sympathy he shows for Moore's certainties, even while criticizing Moore's claims to knowledge, suggests that he moved into a position which made more concessions to realism. Obviously, any attempt to describe the world must avail itself of some system of concepts, but this alone is not sufficient to justify irrealism. There may still be an element of brute fact which imposes a constraint upon all language-games which are played in the interest of attaining truth.

John Wisdom, who had a fondness for metaphors drawn from the hunting field, used to say of philosophers 'We are in at the death'. He was referring primarily to the reduction of philosophy to logical analysis, which he took over-optimistically to be in sight of completion. The metaphor applies more aptly to Wittgenstein's technique, at least as it is displayed in the *Investigations*. If the way out of the fly-bottle were made generally patent, the number of prisoners would become inconsiderable.

In the main I have found myself resisting Wittgenstein's arguments, and am correspondingly disinclined to acquiesce in the limitations which he sought to impose upon philosophy. This does not detract from my appreciation of his brilliance and originality. In these respects I put him second only to Bertrand Russell among the philosophers of the twentieth century.

THE WORKS OF LUDWIG WITTGENSTEIN

I am indebted to Mr Brian McGuinness, Fellow of the Queen's College, Oxford, and to Mr Benjamin Buchan, my editor at Weidenfelds, for the following list of Wittgenstein's published works in chronological order of their composition (with the date of publication in brackets).

Letters to Russell, Keynes and Moore (1974), edited by von Wright and McGuinness.

Notebooks 1914-16 (1961), edited by von Wright and Anscombe.

Vermischte Bemerkungen (*Culture and Value*) (1978, English translation 1980), edited by von Wright.

Prototractatus (1971), edited by McGuinness, Nyberg and von Wright (an early version of the *Tractatus*).

Tractatus Logico-Philosophicus (1922, translation by Ogden and Ramsey; 1961, translation by Pears and McGuinness).

Letters to C.K. Ogden (1973), edited by von Wright.

Letters from Ludwig Wittgenstein, with a memoir by Paul Engelmann (1967), edited by McGuinness.

'Some Remarks on Logical Form', in *Supplementary Proceedings of the Aristotelian Society*, 1929. Also included in Copi and Beard, *Essays on Wittgenstein's Tractatus* (1966).

Philosophische Bemerkungen (*Philosophical Remarks*) (1964, English translation 1975), edited by Rhees.

Philosophische Grammatik (Philosophical Grammar) (1969, English translation 1974), edited by Rhees.

'Ethics', lecture to a Cambridge society in 1929 or 1930, published in *Philosophical Review*, January 1965.

Ludwig Wittgenstein and the Vienna Circle (conversations recorded by F. Waismann) (1979), edited by McGuinness.

G.E. Moore, 'Wittgenstein's Lectures in 1930-33', in *Mind*, vol. 63 (1954) and 64 (1955). Also included in Moore, *Philosophical Papers* (1959).

Wittgenstein's Lectures, Cambridge, 1930-1932 (1980), edited by Lee.

Wittgenstein's Lectures, Cambridge, 1932-1935 (1979), edited by Lee.

The Blue and Brown Books (1958), edited by Rhees.

'Wittgenstein's Notes for Lectures on "Private Experience" and "Sense Data" ', *Philosophical Review*, July 1968.

'Remarks on Frazer's *Golden Bough*', in *Wittgenstein: Sources and Perspectives* (1979), edited by Luckhardt.

Lectures and Conversations on Aesthetics, Psychology and Religious Belief (1966), edited by Barrett (notes of Wittgenstein's classes in 1938 as recorded by some of his students).

'Ursache und Wirkung intuitives Erfassen' (edited by Rhees), in *Philosophia*, vi, 1976.

Lectures on the Foundations of Mathematics (1976), edited by Diamond.

Remarks on the Foundations of Mathematics (1956, revised edn. 1978), edited by von Wright, Rhees and Anscombe.

Philosophical Investigations (1953), edited by Anscombe and Rhees.

Zettel (1967, revised edn. 1981), edited by Anscombe and von Wright.

Remarks on the Philosophy of Psychology (1980, 2 vols.), vol. 1 edited by Anscombe and von Wright, vol. 2 edited by von Wright and Nyman.

On Certainty (1969), edited by Anscombe and von Wright.

Remarks on Colour (1978), edited by Anscombe.

Last Writings on the Philosophy of Psychology, vol. 1 (1982), edited by von Wright and Nyman.

INDEX

About the Author

SIR ALFRED AYER was born in 1910 and educated at Eton College and at Christ Church, Oxford, where he obtained First Class Honours in *Literae Humaniores.* He was Grote Professor of the Philosophy of Mind and Logic at the University of London from 1946 to 1959, and Wykeham Professor of Logic at the University of Oxford from 1959 to 1978. Sir Alfred has been a Fellow of the British Academy since 1952. He holds honorary doctorates from the Universities of Brussels, East Anglia, London and Trent (Ontario). He is an honorary Fellow of University College, London, and, in Oxford, an honorary Fellow of Wadham College and New College, and an honorary student of Christ Church. He is an honorary member of the American Academy of Arts and Sciences and Chevalier of the Légion d'Honneur. He was knighted in 1970. His many published works include *Language, Truth and Logic* (1936, revised edition 1946); *The Foundations of Empirical Knowledge* (1940); *Philosophical Essays* (1954); *The Problem of Knowledge* (1956); *The Concept of a Person and Other Essays* (1963); *The Origins of Pragmatism* (1968); *Metaphysics and Common Sense* (1969); *Russell and Moore: The Analytical Heritage* (1971); *Probability and Evidence* (1972); *Russell* (1972); *The Central Questions of Philosophy* (1973); *Part of My Life* (1977); *Perception and Identity, Essays Presented to A. J. Ayer with His Replies to Them* (1979); *Hume* (1980); *Philosophy in the Twentieth Century* (1982); *Freedom and Morality* (1984); and *More of My Life* (1984); besides articles in philosophical and literary journals.